Tax Policy Reforms 2017

OECD AND SELECTED PARTNER ECONOMIES

This work is published under the responsibility of the Secretary-General of the OECD. The opinions expressed and arguments employed herein do not necessarily reflect the official views of OECD member countries.

This document and any map included herein are without prejudice to the status of or sovereignty over any territory, to the delimitation of international frontiers and boundaries and to the name of any territory, city or area.

Please cite this publication as:
OECD (2017), *Tax Policy Reforms 2017: OECD and Selected Partner Economies*, OECD Publishing, Paris.
http://dx.doi.org/10.1787/9789264279919-en

ISBN 978-92-64-27990-2 (print)
ISBN 978-92-64-27991-9 (PDF)

The statistical data for Israel are supplied by and under the responsibility of the relevant Israeli authorities. The use of such data by the OECD is without prejudice to the status of the Golan Heights, East Jerusalem and Israeli settlements in the West Bank under the terms of international law.

Photo credits: Cover image word cloud ©Tagul.com

Corrigenda to OECD publications may be found on line at: *www.oecd.org/about/publishing/corrigenda.htm*.
© OECD 2017

You can copy, download or print OECD content for your own use, and you can include excerpts from OECD publications, databases and multimedia products in your own documents, presentations, blogs, websites and teaching materials, provided that suitable acknowledgement of OECD as source and copyright owner is given. All requests for public or commercial use and translation rights should be submitted to *rights@oecd.org*. Requests for permission to photocopy portions of this material for public or commercial use shall be addressed directly to the Copyright Clearance Center (CCC) at *info@copyright.com* or the Centre français d'exploitation du droit de copie (CFC) at *contact@cfcopies.com*.

Foreword

This report is the second edition of *Tax Policy Reforms: OECD and Selected Partner Economies*, which is an annual publication that provides comparative information on tax reforms across countries and tracks tax policy developments over time. This year's report covers the tax reforms that were implemented, legislated or announced in 2016. Two non-OECD countries, Argentina and South Africa, have been included in this year's edition, in an effort to progressively expand the scope of the publication to key partner economies. Monitoring tax policy reforms and understanding the context in which they were undertaken is crucial to informing tax policy discussions and to supporting governments in the assessment and design of tax reforms.

This report was produced by the Tax Policy and Statistics Division of the OECD's Centre for Tax Policy and Administration. It was led by Sarah Perret and written jointly with Corinne Luu (Economics Department), Luisa Dressler, Sarita Gomez and Tibor Hanappi (Centre for Tax Policy and Administration), under the supervision of Bert Brys. The authors would like to thank the delegates of Working Party No. 2 on Tax Policy Analysis and Tax Statistics and the Committee on Fiscal Affairs for their inputs. The authors would also like to acknowledge Piet Battiau, Sveinbjorn Blondal, David Bradbury, Giorgia Maffini, Nigel Pain, Alvaro Pereira, Pascal Saint-Amans, Michael Sharratt, Carrie Tyler and Kurt Van Dender, as well as the country desks of the OECD Economics Department for their support and valuable comments.

Table of contents

Editorial 9

Executive summary 11

Chapter 1. **Macroeconomic background** 13

Growth remained subdued in 2016 as a whole, but some signs of improved momentum began to emerge 14
Labour market conditions continued to improve but unemployment remains high in some countries .. 16
Weak investment has contributed to low productivity growth 18
Public debt has stabilised or fallen in many countries... 19
Inequality has continued to rise in the recovery 21
Note 22
References 22

Chapter 2. **Tax revenue trends** 25

Tax-to-GDP ratios varied considerably across OECD countries.. 26
The OECD average tax-to-GDP ratio reached its highest level since the mid-1960s 27
Most countries saw their tax-to-GDP ratios increase between 2014 and 2015 28
The structure of tax revenues continued to shift towards labour and consumption taxes................... 31
Note 32
References 33

Chapter 3. **Tax policy reforms in 2016** 35

3.1. Personal income tax and social security contributions 39
3.2 Corporate income tax and other corporate taxes 53
3.3 VAT/GST and excise duties 65
3.4 Environmentally related taxes 75
3.5 Property taxes... 83
Notes... 86
References 87

Figures

Figure 1.1   Real GDP growth 14
Figure 1.2   The recovery of consumption and investment in OECD countries 15
Figure 1.3   Real GDP growth in OECD countries 15
Figure 1.4   Unemployment rates in OECD countries 16
Figure 1.5   Employment and real income growth.. 17
Figure 1.6   Real private consumption expenditure growth and inflation.................................. 17
Figure 1.7   Real private non-residential gross fixed capital formation growth in OECD countries...... 18
Figure 1.8   Labour productivity in OECD countries since the crisis 19
Figure 1.9   General government gross debt and budget balance.. 20

Figure 1.10   Gross government interest payments in OECD countries 20
Figure 1.11   Market income Gini coefficients 21
Figure 1.12   Market income, post-transfer and disposable income Gini coefficients. 22
Figure 2.1   Tax-to-GDP ratios by country in 2015 26
Figure 2.2   Tax revenues and general government spending as a share of GDP in 2014 (Panel A) and tax revenues as a share of GDP and GDP per capita in 2014 (Panel B) 27
Figure 2.3   Average tax-to-GDP ratio in the OECD, evolution until 2015 28
Figure 2.4   Percentage point changes in tax revenues and government spending as a share of GDP between 2010 and 2015 28
Figure 2.5   Percentage point changes in tax-to-GDP ratios by country between 2014 and 2015 29
Figure 2.6   Percentage point changes in tax-to-GDP ratios by country between 2010 and 2015 30
Figure 2.7   Tax revenue increases between 2010 and 2015 and public debt (Panel A) and tax revenue levels in 2010 (Panel B). 30
Figure 2.8   Evolution of the average tax mix in the OECD, % of total tax revenues 31
Figure 2.9   Tax revenue mixes by country in 2014, % of total tax revenues. 32
Figure 3.1   Budget balances as a share of GDP in countries that introduced fiscal stimulus packages in 2016 39
Figure 3.2   PIT, SSCs and payroll tax revenues as a share of total taxation by country in 2015 40
Figure 3.3   PIT, SSCs and payroll tax revenues as a share of total taxation, OECD average, 1965-2014 40
Figure 3.4   Evolution of the average tax wedge in the OECD between 2000 and 2016 41
Figure 3.5   Changes in labour income tax wedges in OECD countries before and after the financial crisis by family type 42
Figure 3.6   Changes in tax wedge components across OECD countries between 2015 and 2016 42
Figure 3.7   The growth in EOIR relationships created since 2009 50
Figure 3.8   Combined top statutory tax rates on dividend income 52
Figure 3.9   CIT revenues as a share of GDP by country 53
Figure 3.10   Unweighted average CIT rate and CIT revenues in OECD countries, 2000 to 2016 55
Figure 3.11   Standard CIT rates in 2008, 2011 and 2016 and CIT rates on intellectual property 55
Figure 3.12   Changes to central statutory CIT rates implemented or legislated in 2016 56
Figure 3.13   VAT and excise tax revenues as a share of total taxation, OECD average, 1965-2014 66
Figure 3.14   VAT revenues as a share of GDP by country in 2000, 2010 and 2015 66
Figure 3.15   Evolution of the OECD average standard VAT rate until January 2017 66
Figure 3.16   Standard VAT rates by country in 2008 and 2017 67
Figure 3.17   VAT registration or collection thresholds on 1 January 2017 in USD 69
Figure 3.18   VAT Revenue Ratios in OECD countries in 2012 and 2014. 71
Figure 3.19   Revenues from environmentally related taxes as a share of GDP by country in 1995, 2005 and 2014 75
Figure 3.20   Proportion of CO_2 emissions from energy use at different effective carbon rate intervals in EUR per tonne, 2012. 77
Figure 3.21   Taxation across all energy use (weighted average basis), 41 OECD and partner economies, 2012 78
Figure 3.22   Effective tax rates on gasoline and diesel for road use, 2012 79
Figure 3.23   Property tax revenues as a share of GDP by country in 2000 and 2015. 83

Tables

Table 3.1   Expected revenue effects of the tax reforms implemented, legislated or announced in 2016 37
Table 3.2   PIT rate reforms introduced in 2016 44
Table 3.3   PIT base reforms introduced in 2016 46
Table 3.4   Reforms in SSC rates introduced in 2016 48
Table 3.5   Reforms in SSC bases introduced in 2016 49
Table 3.6   Changes to tax rates on capital income introduced in 2016 51
Table 3.7   Changes to capital income tax bases introduced in 2016 51
Table 3.8   CIT rate changes introduced in 2016 56

Table 3.9	CIT base changes introduced in 2016	59
Table 3.10	Changes to standard VAT rates introduced in 2016	68
Table 3.11	Changes to reduced VAT rates introduced in 2016	69
Table 3.12	Changes to VAT registration/collection thresholds introduced in 2016	70
Table 3.13	Excise tax increases on alcohol and tobacco products introduced in 2016	73
Table 3.14	Changes to excise taxes on soft drinks introduced in 2016	74
Table 3.15	Changes to taxes on energy use implemented, legislated or announced in 2016	77
Table 3.16	Changes to taxes on motor vehicles and other transport taxes implemented, legislated or announced in 2016	81
Table 3.17	Changes to other environmentally related taxes implemented, legislated or announced in 2016	82
Table 3.18	Property tax reforms that were implemented, legislated or announced in 2016	84

Boxes

Box 3.1	The OECD Annual Tax Policy Reform Questionnaire	36
Box 3.2	Changes in labour income tax progressivity	43
Box 3.3	The exchange of information on tax matters and tackling tax evasion	50
Box 3.4	Luxembourg's comprehensive tax reform	57
Box 3.5	Hungary's package of tax reforms	58
Box 3.6	Recommended policy measures to address BEPS	63
Box 3.7	Environmental tax subsidy reform in Mexico	80

Editorial

Growth has been slowly picking up and this is welcome news. But countries are still facing a vicious circle of low productivity growth, sluggish demand, stagnant wages and, in many countries, rising or high levels of inequalities. Over the decade since the financial crisis, the OECD has become increasingly concerned about the persistent inequalities in growth, income, and wealth within and between countries and has encouraged a shift from a narrow focus on economic growth towards a greater emphasis on inclusiveness. Indeed, ensuring that growth is broad-based and does not leave large sections of the population behind is crucial to future economic and social prosperity.

The design of tax systems plays a key role in supporting economic growth and in ensuring that the benefits of growth are shared more widely. Tax policies raise the revenues needed to support the public investments and programmes that will help foster growth and inclusiveness. Progressive taxation is central to income redistribution and can help reduce wealth inequalities. Tax policies also affect taxpayers' behaviours and incentives to work, consume, save and invest, which in turn have significant effects on both growth and equity. Finally, maintaining the integrity of our tax systems so that citizens are confident that all individuals and businesses are making a contribution and that the tax laws are being applied fairly to all is essential to ensuring continued trust in and support for our institutions.

Against this backdrop, both OECD and its partner economies have continued to place growth and inclusiveness at the heart of their tax reform efforts over the last year. Growth-oriented tax reforms have enhanced the investment climate by reducing taxes on businesses and lowered income tax burdens on individuals. This development is largely positive as corporate and labour income taxes, which have both been identified empirically as the most harmful to growth, are being reduced and, over time, these efforts are being accompanied by a gradual shift towards less economically distortive taxes including VAT, excise duties, property taxes and environmentally related taxes. Reforms aimed at fostering inclusiveness have focused on lowering personal income taxes on low and middle income earners and on families and, in some countries, on shifting the tax burden on capital income from the corporate to the personal level, which is likely to have positive effects on both equity and growth. Tax reforms that contribute to strengthening progressivity and redistribution will play a key role in addressing today's high levels of income and wealth inequality and in bridging the divide between those who have benefited from growth and those who have not.

Countries have also made significant progress on OECD-led initiatives aimed at ensuring that companies and individuals pay their fair share of taxes. Efforts to protect corporate tax bases against international tax avoidance have continued, in line with the commitments made by countries to implement the minimum standards and recommendations agreed upon as part of the OECD/G20 Base Erosion and Profit Shifting (BEPS) project. Continued progress on the Exchange of Information on Request as well as the introduction of the Automatic Exchange of Information also mark a step change in the area of tax transparency. Finally, major improvements have been achieved regarding the application of VAT in the digital sector, with an increasing number of countries aligning their tax rules on cross-border supplies of services and intangibles with the *OECD International VAT/GST Guidelines*.

However, some of the recent tax policy trends identified in this report pose important questions that will need to be considered closely. An increase in corporate tax rate competition, after a period of relative stabilisation in the years immediately following the crisis, raises challenging questions for governments seeking to strike the right balance between maintaining a competitive tax system and ensuring they continue to raise the revenues necessary to fund vital public services, social programmes and infrastructure. In the area of environmentally related taxes, the fact that taxes on transport fuels were increased further, while fuels in other sectors that have detrimental environmental and health effects remain taxed at very low rates, also raises concern. With regard to labour taxation, despite cuts in personal income taxes, social security contributions remain high in many countries and this will require further action if the overall tax burden on labour income is to be reduced and incentives to work enhanced.

Ongoing work to monitor and compare tax policy reforms over time and across a wide range of countries, both in OECD members and in key partner economies, is crucial to informing tax policy discussions and supporting governments in the assessment and design of reforms. It will help ensure that future tax policies play their role in supporting growth, fairness and environmental sustainability.

Angel Gurría
OECD Secretary-General

Executive summary

This report is the second edition of *Tax Policy Reforms: OECD and Selected Partner Economies*, which is an annual publication that provides comparative information on tax reforms across countries and tracks tax policy developments over time. The report covers the tax policy reforms that were implemented, legislated or announced during calendar year 2016 in all OECD countries as well as in Argentina and South Africa.

The report is structured as follows: Chapter 1 describes the macroeconomic environment from the end of the crisis until 2016; Chapter 2 presents the latest trends in tax revenues and tax mixes in OECD countries, Argentina and South Africa; and Chapter 3 gives an overview of the main tax policy developments and tax reform trends in each category of tax in 2016.

The report shows that low growth rates in conjunction with improvements in public budgets have pushed many countries to continue introducing growth-oriented tax reforms. Numerous reforms have sought to encourage investment, in particular through reductions in corporate income tax (CIT) rates. Fiscal stimulus was also provided to individuals through personal income tax (PIT) reductions. While most CIT and PIT reforms are expected to have negative effects on revenues, many countries are anticipating revenue increases from VAT, excise duties, property taxes and environmentally related taxes which are generally considered less detrimental to economic growth than direct taxes.

Other important motivations behind tax reforms included enhancing fairness and deterring harmful consumption. The numerous PIT cuts targeted at low and middle income earners, in addition to supporting growth, were a response to low income growth, especially at the bottom of the income distribution, while many of the increases in excise duties and environmentally related taxes were aimed at deterring harmful behaviours and consumption.

This year's report identified a number of important tax reform trends:

- Personal income taxes on low and middle income earners have been reduced in a number of countries, but the impact of these tax cuts on redistribution and overall tax wedges is expected to be limited. The PIT reforms introduced in 2016 have generally lowered PIT rates and narrowed tax bases, in particular for low and middle-income earners. However, most of the PIT reforms are expected to have negative revenue effects, meaning that despite greater progressivity, the overall redistributive impact of PITs might not necessarily increase. In addition, while tax wedges are expected to be further reduced – especially for low-wage earners – as a consequence of recent PIT reforms, social security contributions (SSCs) continue to remain high in many countries.

- In relation to corporate income taxes, there has been continuing progress on the implementation of BEPS related measures and we have also seen competition on corporate tax rates intensifying. On the one hand, efforts to protect corporate tax bases against international tax avoidance continued, in line with countries' commitments to implement the minimum standards and recommendations agreed upon as part of the OECD/G20 Base Erosion and Profit Shifting (BEPS) project. On the other hand, we have seen an intensification of competition on CIT rates, which had already been identified as an emerging trend last year, after a period of relative stabilisation in the years immediately after the crisis. Many of the countries that lowered their CIT rates have done so through multi-year cuts, but there were a few exceptions, most notably Hungary which introduced a very significant and sudden CIT rate reduction. This year's report also points to increasing tax competition through new or enhanced tax incentives, in particular for research and development (R&D) and intellectual property (IP)-related activities.

- Countries have stopped increasing standard VAT rates to raise additional revenue and the most significant area of reform in the last year has been regarding the application of VAT in the digital sector. Apart from Greece which raised its standard VAT rate, there were no changes to standard VAT rates in 2016, suggesting that the willingness of countries to raise additional revenues through increases in the standard VAT rate has diminished, in part because these rates have already reached high levels in many countries. One of the most significant evolutions in the area of VAT has been the increasing number of countries aligning their tax rules on cross-border supplies of services and intangibles with the OECD International VAT/GST Guidelines.

- A large number of countries reported excise duty increases, as a way to simultaneously raise revenues and influence consumer behaviour. Excise duty increases on tobacco products were particularly numerous. Reported reforms and future reform plans also confirmed the increasing popularity of taxes on soft drinks in many countries.

- In the area of environmentally related taxes, the recent trend that has seen taxes on transport fuels increase continued in many countries. This differs from fuels in other sectors which, despite also causing considerable harm to the climate, the environment and human health, often remain taxed at very low rates. There were also a number of reforms related to vehicle taxes, generally involving increased taxes on conventional fuel vehicles and expanded tax incentives for alternative fuel vehicles.

- There were more changes reported in the area of property taxes than last year and these reforms were often aimed at raising taxes. The taxes that were raised generally included recurrent taxes on immovable property as well as transaction taxes on both movable and immovable property. Some reforms related to real estate taxation sought to "cool" housing markets by targeting investment in housing. Inheritance tax reforms, on the other hand, mostly involved tax reductions.

The countries undertaking the most wide-ranging reforms were predominantly members of the European Union (EU), with Austria, Belgium, Greece, Hungary, Luxembourg, the Netherlands and Norway being identified as having introduced the most comprehensive tax reforms in 2016. With the exception of Greece, which continued its efforts to meet the fiscal targets under its third bailout programme, comprehensive tax reform packages were aimed at supporting growth, in particular through reductions in taxes on labour and corporate income. Reflecting the fact that reforms were generally growth oriented, all the countries that introduced comprehensive tax reforms except Greece are expecting negative revenue effects, at least in the short run. Revenue estimations also show that comprehensive labour tax reforms are expected to be much more costly than comprehensive corporate tax reforms.

Chapter 1

Macroeconomic background

This chapter gives an overview of the main macroeconomic trends from the end of the crisis until 2016. The purpose of this overview is to provide background information to help understand tax revenue trends as well as tax policy changes. Tax policy reforms are closely connected with economic trends: tax revenues are affected by changes in macroeconomic conditions and economic trends themselves are key drivers of tax reforms.

The statistical data for Israel are supplied by and under the responsibility of the relevant Israeli authorities. The use of such data by the OECD is without prejudice to the status of the Golan Heights, East Jerusalem and Israeli settlements in the West Bank under the terms of international law.

The macroeconomic background covers recent trends in growth, consumption, investment, productivity, the labour market, inflation, public finances and inequality. Tax policy developments are closely connected with economic trends: tax revenues are affected by changes in macroeconomic conditions and economic trends themselves are key drivers of tax reforms. This chapter provides background information to help understand the tax revenue trends and the tax policy changes that are discussed in Chapters 2 and 3.

Growth remained subdued in 2016 as a whole, but some signs of improved momentum began to emerge

Global GDP growth remained subdued for the fifth successive year in 2016, at around 3%, well below the average of around 4% seen in the two decades prior to the financial crisis. Since the crisis, persistent growth shortfalls have weighed on future output expectations, holding back current spending and potential output growth. Weak demand has been reflected in subdued investment and global trade, in turn limiting the advances in labour productivity and wages that are required to sustain higher consumption and output growth. However, some signs of improving momentum have now begun to emerge, with rising business and consumer confidence in most economies. A modest global cyclical upturn began to be reflected in output and trade growth towards the end of 2016, and continued into early 2017 (OECD, 2017b).

The further easing of global growth in 2016 as a whole largely reflected softer outcomes in the OECD economies, especially in the first half of the year, with growth improving in the non-OECD countries after an extended post-crisis slowdown (Figure 1.1). The growth pick-up in the non-OECD economies was helped by stronger policy-supported infrastructure investment in Asia, especially China, and the gradual easing of recessions in many commodity producers, including Brazil and Russia, alongside improvements in commodity prices. Growth in China moderated only slightly in 2016, as a result of stepped-up policy support, and the transition towards consumption and services continued, with adjustments to oversupply in heavy industries and real estate. In 2015 and 2016, global trade volumes rose only slightly faster than global output, rather than nearly twice as fast as in the pre-crisis

Figure 1.1. **Real GDP growth**
Year-on-year percentage changes

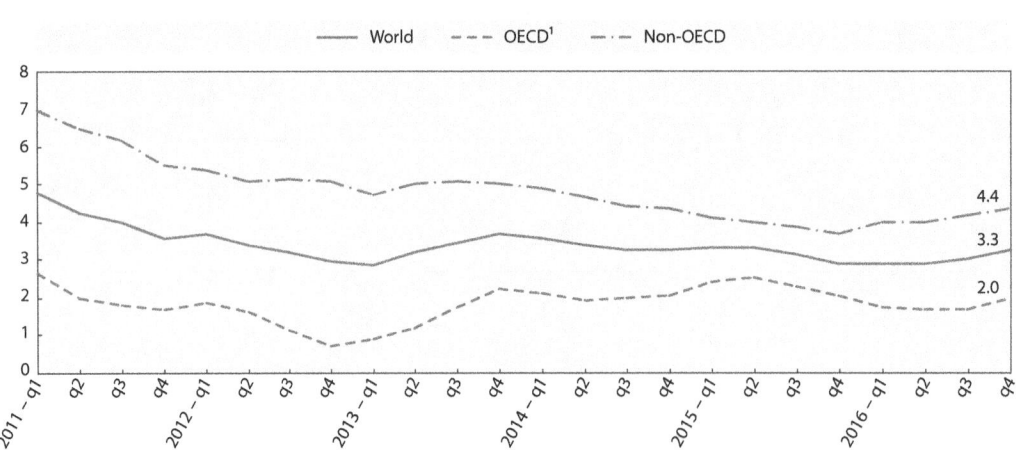

Note: GDP measured using purchasing power parities. 1. With growth in Ireland in 2015 computed using gross value added at constant prices excluding foreign-owned multinational enterprise dominated sectors.

Source: OECD Economic Outlook 101 database.

years. Structural factors, including a slowdown in trade liberalisation and a contraction of global value chains, along with the cyclical weakness of investment, all held down trade growth (Haugh et al., 2016). However, global trade growth and investment showed some improvement in the second half of 2016, particularly in Asia and Europe.

The recovery in the OECD economies since the global financial crisis has been modest compared to past recoveries, with weak consumption and investment (Figure 1.2). Growth in the OECD economies moderated to 1.8% in 2016, around ¼ percentage point weaker than in the previous two years. Growth dynamics amongst the OECD economies were mixed in 2016, with improvements in the large euro area countries and Japan relative to the previous two years, but weaker growth in North America and the United Kingdom (Figure 1.3).

Figure 1.2. **The recovery of consumption and investment in OECD countries**

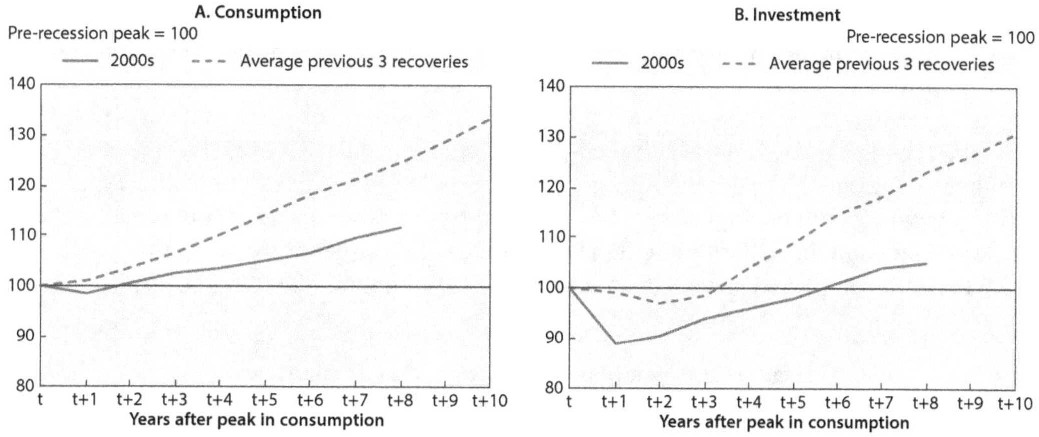

Note: Aggregate data for the OECD economies. Consumption is total consumers' expenditure and investment is total gross fixed capital formation. The average of the past three recoveries is an unweighted average of developments after 1973Q4, 1980Q1, 1990Q3 and 2008Q1. Series scaled to equal 100 in these quarters. All data are at constant prices.

Source: OECD Economic Outlook 101 database.

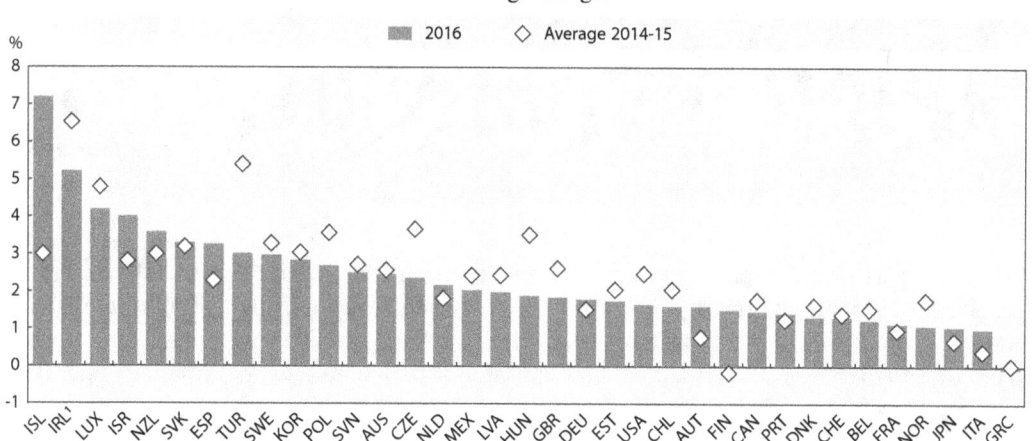

Figure 1.3. **Real GDP growth in OECD countries**
Percentage changes

Note: 1. With growth in Ireland in 2015 computed using gross value added at constant prices excluding foreign-owned multinational enterprise dominated sectors.

Source: OECD Economic Outlook 101 database.

The expansion in the United States was boosted by employment gains, improved confidence and wealth effects, which have sustained consumption growth, despite headwinds from the stronger dollar and weak business investment. Growth in the euro area was supported by increasingly-accommodative monetary policy and an end to area-wide fiscal consolidation, although high non-performing loans and labour market slack continued to hold back demand in some countries. In Japan, additional monetary easing helped to support domestic demand, and the recovery of world trade in late 2016 contributed to an improvement in external demand.

Labour market conditions continued to improve but unemployment remains high in some countries

Labour market conditions improved further in 2016, with unemployment rates generally continuing to moderate from post-recession peaks. However, the level of unemployment remained elevated in some countries, particularly in the euro area (Figure 1.4). In the OECD as a whole, the unemployment rate stood at 5.8% in 2017Q1, below the post-crisis peak of 8.5% seen in late 2009 but still ¼ percentage point above its pre-crisis level. Despite this progress, long-term and youth unemployment and the number of involuntary part-time workers remain elevated. Still-high long-term unemployment increases the risk of a rising number of discouraged workers – people who drop out of the labour force and experience skills attrition. Youth unemployment has declined from post-crisis peaks but remains above pre-crisis levels in the majority of OECD countries, with a larger share of youth classified as NEET (neither employed nor in education or training) than in 2007 (OECD, 2016c).

Figure 1.4. **Unemployment rates in OECD countries**

As a percentage of the labour force

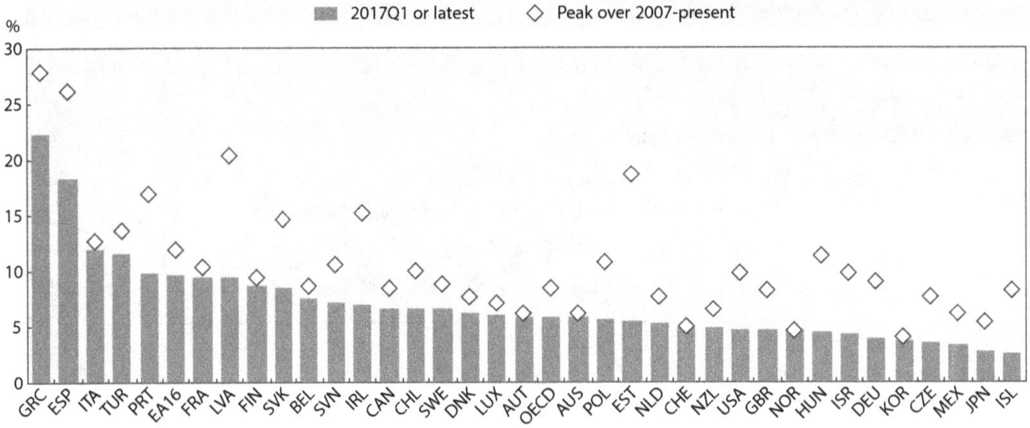

Source: OECD Economic Outlook 101 database; and OECD calculations.

In 2016 as whole, employment growth picked up in the majority of OECD countries, despite subdued output growth (Figure 1.5, Panel A). Moreover, in roughly half of the OECD countries, employment rates (relative to the population aged 15-74) have moved above levels seen prior to the crisis. Nevertheless, the share of part-time employment remains higher than pre-crisis levels in the majority of OECD countries (OECD, 2017b), and the number of hours worked per employee has declined. Wage growth remained subdued in the major advanced economies in 2016 (Figure 1.5, Panel B), in part reflecting weak productivity growth as well as continuing cyclical slack in labour markets.

Figure 1.5. **Employment and real income growth**
Year-on-year percentage changes

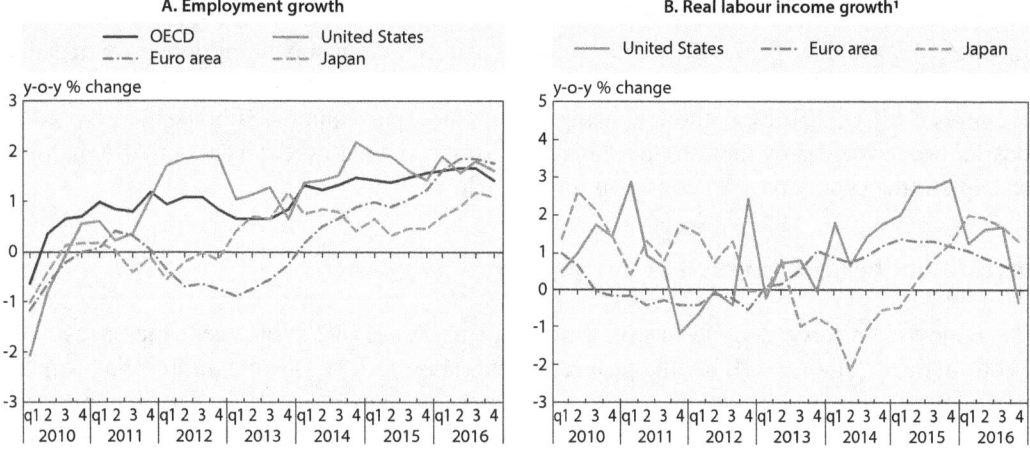

Note: 1. Labour income per employee deflated by the private consumption deflator.

Source: OECD Economic Outlook 101 database.

Moderating income gains with rising commodity prices has checked consumption growth since mid-2016

After falling in 2015, commodity prices trended upward through 2016, improving the growth outlook for commodity producers and the revenue raising capacity of governments in commodity-exporting economies. Oil prices were further boosted in late 2016, following the OPEC agreement in November 2016 to cut oil production, while metals prices were also higher in the second half of 2016, supported by rising global industrial production and increased demand from China following policy stimulus. Commodity-importing economies faced rising import costs and input price inflation since mid-2016. Headline inflation rose in most countries starting in mid-2016 as a result of higher energy prices (Figure 1.6, Panel A),

Figure 1.6. **Real private consumption expenditure growth and inflation**
Year-on-year percentage changes

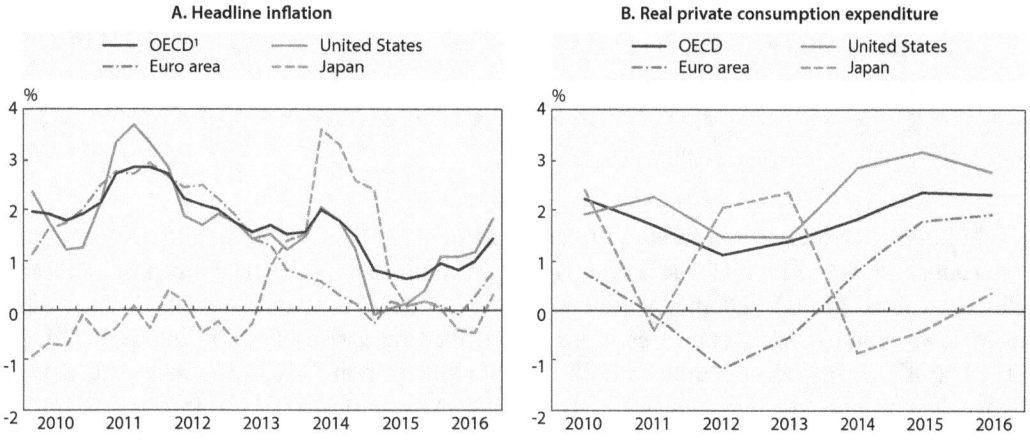

Note: 1. OECD aggregate is computed based on different indicators: United States: price index for personal consumption expenditure; euro area members and United Kingdom: harmonised index of consumer prices; and other countries: national consumer price index.

Source: OECD Economic Outlook 101 database.

which reduced household purchasing power, at least temporarily. However, underlying inflation remained subdued.

Private consumption moderated in the major economies and for the OECD as a whole in 2016 (Figure 1.6, Panel B). Cross-country differences in consumption growth since the crisis are closely associated with differences in real income growth, especially labour incomes (OECD, 2016b). Although rising employment has supported household incomes, despite weak wage growth, household income growth slowed in real terms in 2016, helping to explain the slower pace of consumption growth.

Weak investment has contributed to low productivity growth

Following a large decline in investment during the crisis, subsequent increases have been subdued, lagging well behind past recoveries (Figure 1.2). Despite improving business confidence, private investment growth generally remained weak in OECD countries in 2016 and was below the averages seen since 2010 in some of them (Figure 1.7). This weakness reflected persistent soft domestic and global demand, elevated uncertainty and financial constraints arising from impaired banking sectors in some economies. Fiscal consolidation has also constrained public fixed investment in many countries. Moreover, the structural shift from high investment-intensive industrial sectors to less investment-intensive services has continued in some advanced economies (OECD, 2015a).

Figure 1.7. **Real private non-residential gross fixed capital formation growth in OECD countries**
Percentage changes

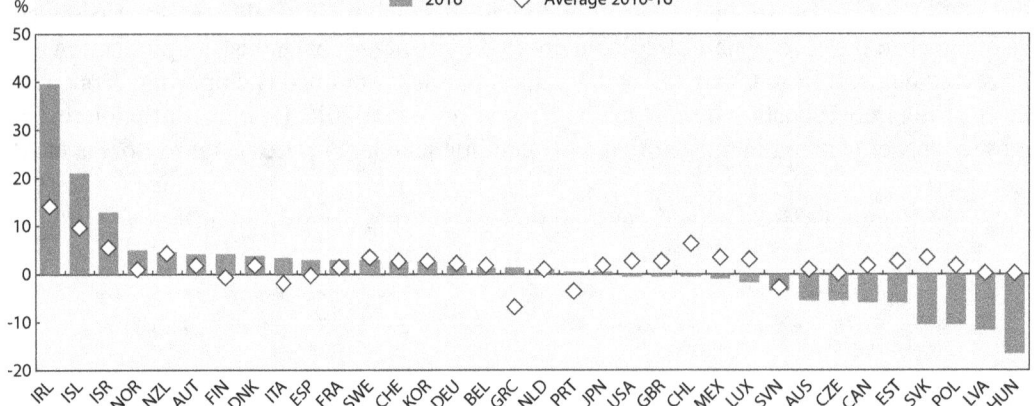

Source: OECD Economic Outlook 101 database.

Following an increase in foreign direct investment (FDI) in 2015, data for 2016 suggest a partial reversal in FDI inflows, driven largely by a fall to non-OECD countries, including China. Annual global FDI inflows were down 7% in 2016, with a decline of over 18% in inflows to non-OECD countries more than offsetting a rise of 6% in inflows into the OECD (OECD, 2017d). Just under a half of the decline to non-OECD countries was driven by weaker inflows to China. The total inward FDI stock in the OECD countries rose by 5½ per cent in 2016, representing over three-fifths of the estimated global FDI stock.

Weak investment, in conjunction with the trade slowdown and reduced structural policy ambition, has contributed to sluggish labour productivity growth by slowing the increase in productive capital per worker, as well as the diffusion of new ideas and technology embodied in new equipment. Labour productivity growth in OECD countries since the crisis has generally fallen significantly below that seen in the decade prior to the crisis, checking future potential growth (Figure 1.8). Moreover, in the post-crisis period, there has been relatively weak growth in multi-factor productivity, which reflects the efficiency with which inputs are used (OECD, 2015b). Productivity gaps between firms have widened as frontier firms have continued to make gains but laggard firms have under-performed, contributing to the widening gap in real incomes and rising inequality (Andrews et al., 2016). These trends have led to low income growth for many households, particularly at the bottom of the income distribution and have in turn held back aggregate consumption growth.

Figure 1.8. **Labour productivity in OECD countries since the crisis**
Percentage changes

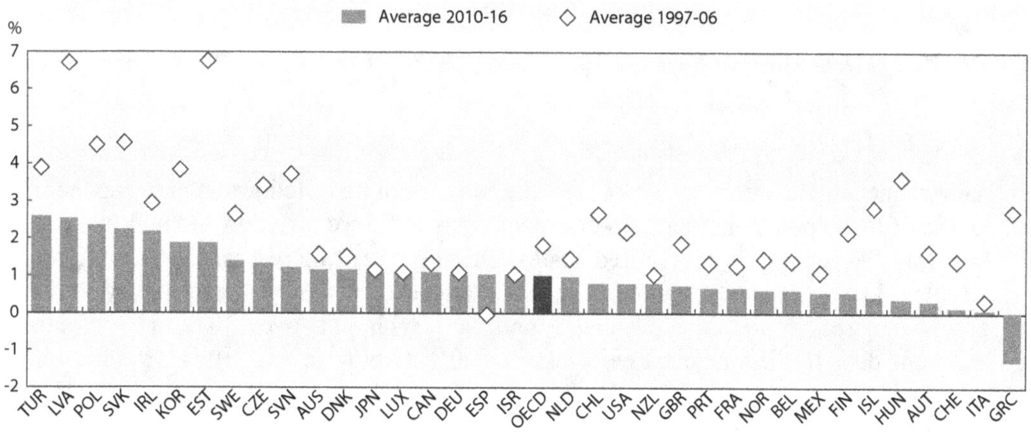

Note: 1. With growth in Ireland in 2015 computed using gross value added at constant prices excluding foreign-owned multinational enterprise dominated sectors.

Source: OECD Economic Outlook 101 database.

Public debt has stabilised or fallen in many countries

After reaching high levels in the aftermath of the financial crisis, general government gross debt as a share of GDP has begun to stabilise in the OECD area (Figure 1.9), and euro area economies have seen some declines, on average, over the past two years. The average OECD gross debt-to-GDP ratio stood at about 113% in 2016, up from 97% in 2010. Across the OECD, there were wide differences between countries, with gross general government financial liabilities ranging from 13% of GDP in Estonia to 222% in Japan in 2016.

Budget deficits in OECD countries have shrunk as a share of GDP since peaking in 2009 (Figure 1.9, Panel B). On average across OECD countries, the budget deficit dropped to 3% of GDP in 2016, compared with 8.4% in 2009. In 2016, there was a wide difference between OECD countries, with budget surpluses in Germany and Korea and a sizeable deficit in the United States and Japan. The slight decline in the underlying primary balance[1] in OECD countries suggests the fiscal stance has generally become moderately expansionary since 2015 after several years of budgetary consolidation. Moreover, further expansionary fiscal measures have been announced in some large OECD countries in 2017-18, with very-low long-term interest rates providing space for new fiscal initiatives (Botev et al., 2016).

Figure 1.9. **General government gross debt and budget balance**
As a percentage of GDP

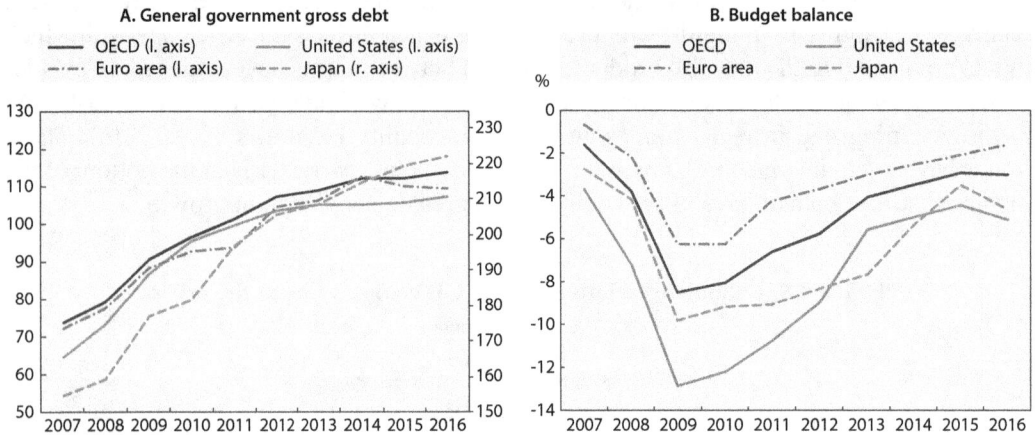

Source: OECD Economic Outlook 101 database.

Government bond yields have however turned up from historic lows in many economies since mid-2016, helped by higher market expectations of future inflation and nominal policy interest rates, especially in the United States. Despite recent increases, long-term interest rates remain low by historical standards, reflecting the exceptional monetary policy stimulus measures undertaken in the advanced economies, with just over 30% of outstanding government debt trading at negative yields in 2016 (Botev et al., 2016). In addition to conventional and unconventional monetary easing, which have compressed term premiums, debt servicing costs have also been lowered by declining risk spreads, the extension of debt maturities and fiscal consolidation in some countries (Botev et al., 2016). As shown in Figure 1.10, gross government interest payments as a share of GDP are generally below levels seen following the crisis in OECD countries, despite higher debt levels, increasing fiscal space in many countries.

Figure 1.10. **Gross government interest payments in OECD countries**
As a percentage of GDP

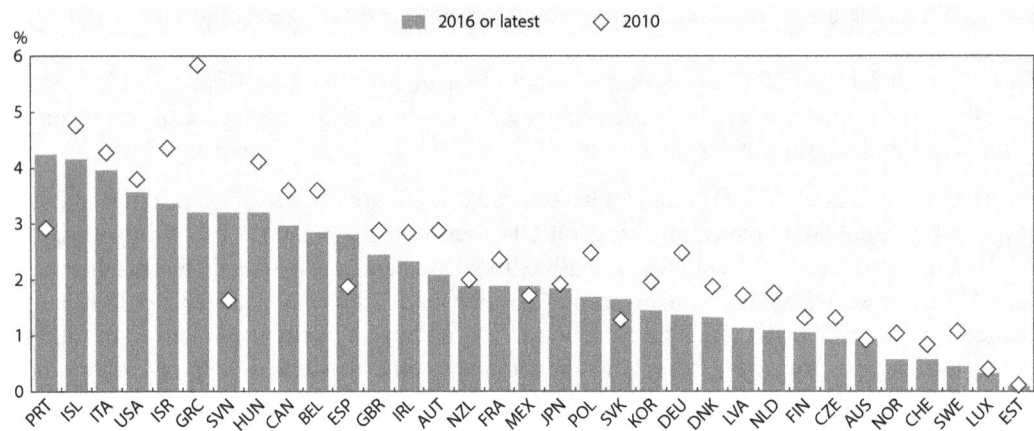

Source: OECD Economic Outlook 101 database; and OECD calculations.

Inequality has continued to rise in the recovery

Inequality in OECD countries remains high by historical standards. The continued rise in income inequality in some countries has compounded the drag on economy-wide household spending from weak income growth, as the higher-income households in which income growth has been concentrated typically have a lower marginal propensity to consume. While cross-country patterns of income inequality depend to some extent on how inequality is measured, the most widely used measure is the Gini coefficient (OECD, 2017a). Inequality of market incomes (i.e. before taxes and transfers) has continued to increase slightly since the financial crisis on average in OECD countries, with 20 out of 33 countries with available data reporting an increase (Figure 1.11). The extent of the change in market income inequality since 2010 has varied widely across countries (Figure 1.11), with the largest increase seen in Greece (8%) and the largest fall in Turkey (-12%). At the OECD level, the Gini coefficient on market incomes (based on the working-age population), was up only slightly (+0.7%) compared with 2010.

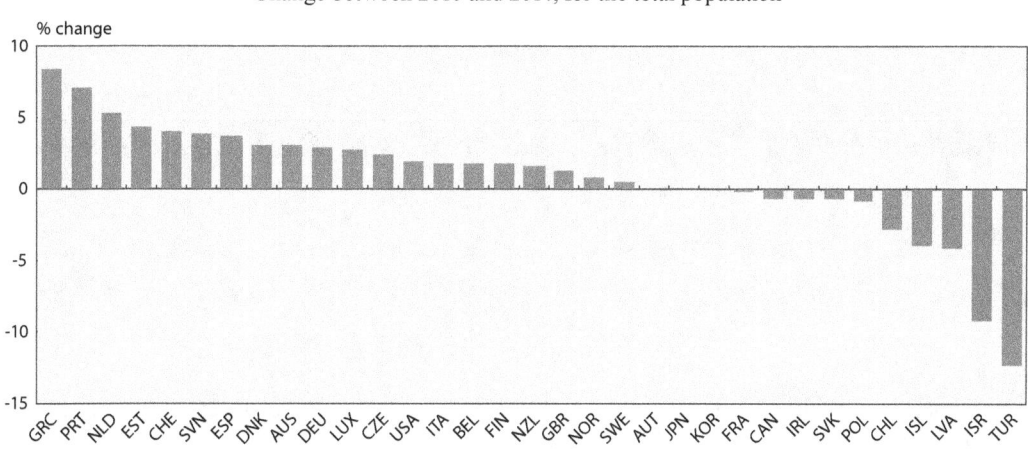

Figure 1.11. **Market income Gini coefficients**
Change between 2010 and 2014, for the total population

Note: Most recent figures are used.

Source: OECD Income Distribution Database (IDD).

On average in OECD countries, taxes and transfers reduce income inequality by just over a quarter; of this, over two-thirds are due to transfers and the remaining portion is due to taxes (Figure 1.12). There are considerable differences amongst countries, with the largest redistribution through taxes and transfers found in Ireland (41%) and the weakest in Mexico (0.3%). The impact of redistribution is even higher if non-cash transfers from governments, such as education and healthcare, are taken into account (OECD, 2016a). Nonetheless, the extent of redistribution via taxes and transfers has tended to decline in roughly two-thirds of OECD countries since 2010, adding to the pressures on income distributions from developments in market incomes. This may reflect a reduction in transfers as part of fiscal consolidation and reduced progressivity of the tax system.

At the OECD level, the average Gini coefficient of disposable household income (which takes account of taxes and transfers as well as gross income) increased by 1% from 2010 to 2013/14, reaching 0.318. While the recovery since 2010 improved average disposable incomes, the more rapid growth of top incomes (2.3%) and a weaker improvement at the bottom and at the middle (1.1% and 1.3%) contributed to increasing inequality (OECD, 2016a). By 2013/14, incomes at the bottom of the distribution were still well below pre-crisis levels, while top and middle incomes had recovered much of the ground lost during the crisis. In around half of the major emerging market economies, disposable income inequality has decreased since the mid-2000s, including in Brazil, Turkey, South Africa and China (OECD, 2017a; 2017c). However, increases were reported in India and Russia.

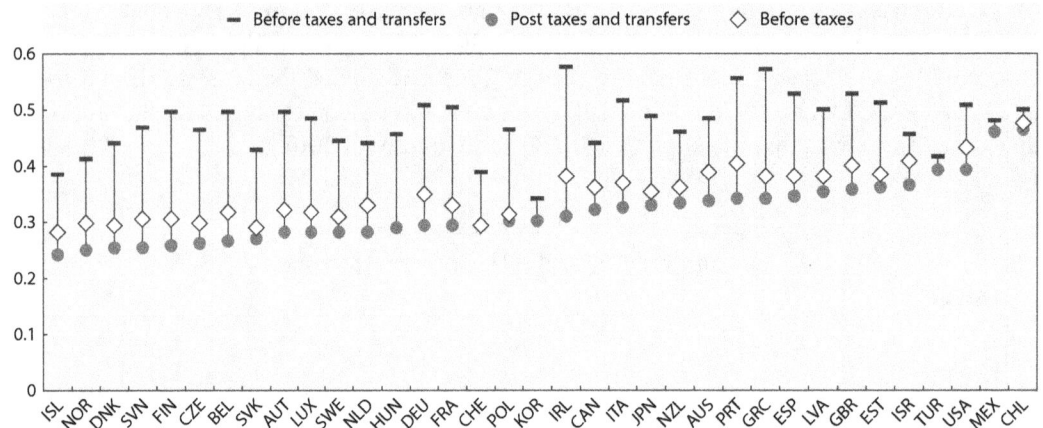

Figure 1.12. **Market income, post-transfer and disposable income Gini coefficients**
2014 or latest, for total population

Source: OECD Income Distribution Database (IDD).

Note

1. The underlying primary balance is the fiscal balance excluding net interest payments and adjusted for the economic cycle and for budgetary one-offs.

References

Andrews, D., C. Criscuolo and P. Gal (2016), "The Global Productivity Slowdown, Technology Divergence and Public Policy: A Firm Level Perspective", *Brookings Institution Hutchins Center Working Papers*, No. 24.

Botev, J., J. Fournier and A. Mourougane (2016), "A Re-assessment of Fiscal Space in OECD Countries", *OECD Economics Department Working Papers*, No. 1352, OECD Publishing, Paris, http://dx.doi.org/10.1787/fec60e1b-en.

Haugh, D., et al. (2016), "Cardiac Arrest or Dizzy Spell: Why is World Trade So Weak and What can Policy Do About It?", *OECD Economic Policy Papers*, No. 18, OECD Publishing, Paris, http://dx.doi.org/10.1787/5jlr2h45q532-en.

OECD (2017a), *Economic Policy Reforms 2017: Going for Growth*, OECD Publishing, Paris, http://dx.doi.org/10.1787/growth-2017-en.

OECD (2017b), *OECD Economic Outlook*, Volume 2017 Issue 1, OECD Publishing, Paris, http://dx.doi.org/10.1787/eco_outlook-v2017-1-en.

OECD (2017c), *OECD Economic Surveys: China 2017*, OECD Publishing, Paris, http://dx.doi.org/10.1787/eco_surveys-chn-2017-en.

OECD (2017d), *FDI in Figures*, April 2017, OECD Publishing, Paris. www.oecd.org/daf/inv/investment-policy/FDI-in-Figures-April-2017.pdf (accessed 1 July 2017).

OECD (2016a), "Inequality Update – November 2016", OECD Publishing, Paris, www.oecd.org/social/OECD2016-Income-Inequality-Update.pdf (accessed 1 July 2017).

OECD (2016b), *OECD Economic Outlook, Volume 2016 Issue 2*, OECD Publishing, Paris, http://dx.doi.org/10.1787/eco_outlook-v2016-2-en.

OECD (2016c), *OECD Employment Outlook 2016*, OECD Publishing, Paris, http://dx.doi.org/10.1787/empl_outlook-2016-en.

OECD (2015a), *OECD Economic Outlook*, Volume 2015 Issue 1, OECD Publishing, Paris, http://dx.doi.org/10.1787/eco_outlook-v2015-1-en.

OECD (2015b), *The Future of Productivity*, OECD Publishing, Paris, http://dx.doi.org/10.1787/9789264248533-en.

Chapter 2

Tax revenue trends

This chapter describes tax revenue trends – looking at both total tax-to-GDP ratios and tax mixes – in OECD countries, Argentina and South Africa. The analysis covers tax revenue trends until 2015, the latest year for which comparable tax revenue data is available. This overview of tax revenue trends is useful to understand the effects of past tax policy reforms and sets the stage for the subsequent discussion on the tax reforms that were introduced in 2016.

The statistical data for Israel are supplied by and under the responsibility of the relevant Israeli authorities. The use of such data by the OECD is without prejudice to the status of the Golan Heights, East Jerusalem and Israeli settlements in the West Bank under the terms of international law.

This chapter describes tax revenue trends – looking at both total tax-to-GDP ratios and tax mixes – in OECD countries, Argentina and South Africa. The analysis covers tax revenue trends until 2015, the latest year for which comparable tax revenue data is available (OECD, 2016a). This overview of tax revenue trends is useful to understand the effects of past tax policy reforms and sets the stage for the subsequent discussion on the tax reforms that were introduced in 2016.

Overall, this chapter shows that tax revenues as a share of GDP have increased in a majority of OECD countries between 2014 and 2015 and that the OECD average tax-to-GDP ratio reached a new historical record in 2015. In addition, the composition of tax revenues has on average continued to shift towards labour taxes and VAT. These tax revenue trends partly reflect the adoption of active fiscal consolidation measures – and in many cases of reforms aimed at raising PIT, SSCs and VAT – in the years that followed the crisis (OECD, 2016b).

Tax-to-GDP ratios varied considerably across OECD countries

Tax revenues as a share of GDP varied significantly across countries. In 2015, Denmark had the highest tax-to-GDP ratio among all the countries covered in the report – including OECD countries, Argentina and South Africa – reaching 46.6%, followed by France (45.5%) and Belgium (44.8%). On the other hand, Mexico (17.4% in 2015) and Chile (20.7%) had the lowest tax-to-GDP ratios. They were followed by Ireland, which had the third lowest ratio at 23.6%, and Korea at 25.3% (Figure 2.1).

Figure 2.1. **Tax-to-GDP ratios by country in 2015**

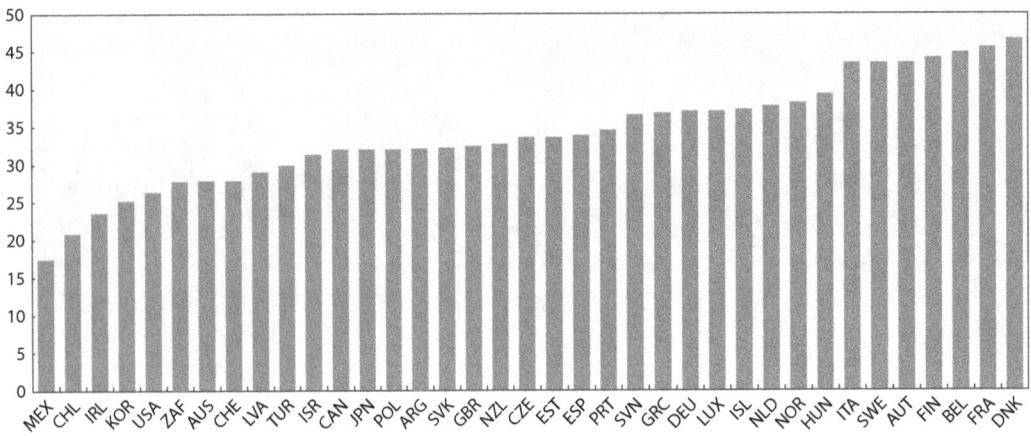

Note: 2014 data for Australia, Japan, Poland and South Africa.

Source: Regional Revenue Statistics databases (www.oecd.org/tax/tax-policy/revenue-statistics-comparable-tax-revenue-data.htm).

Countries' tax-to-GDP ratios are unsurprisingly very closely associated with their levels of government spending. As may be expected, countries with high tax-to-GDP ratios tend to be the ones that also report high levels of general government expenditure as a share of GDP (Figure 2.2, Panel A).

There is also a slightly positive correlation between tax-to-GDP ratios and GDP per capita. Figure 2.2 (Panel B) shows that tax revenues as a share of GDP tend to be higher in countries with higher GDP per capita. This correlation is more pronounced when the comparison includes countries with lower levels of GDP per capita which are not shown here (see for instance OECD, 2016c). However, different groups of countries can be distinguished: higher tax-to-GDP ratio and higher GDP per capita countries (including for instance Scandinavian countries, Austria, Belgium and France); lower tax-to-GDP ratio and higher GDP per capita countries (Anglo-Saxon countries, Korea, Japan); lower tax-to-GDP ratio and lower GDP per capita countries (in particular emerging countries such as Mexico, Chile, Turkey and South Africa); and higher tax-to-GDP ratio and lower GDP per capita countries (some Central and Southern European countries).

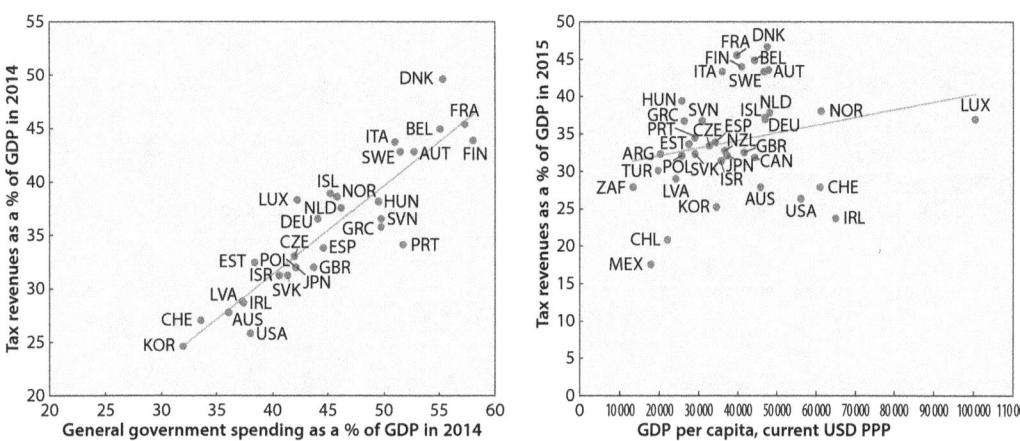

Figure 2.2. **Tax revenues and general government spending as a share of GDP in 2014 (Panel A) and tax revenues as a share of GDP and GDP per capita in 2014 (Panel B)**

Source: OECD Economic Outlook 100 database and Regional Revenue Statistics databases (www.oecd.org/tax/tax-policy/revenue-statistics-comparable-tax-revenue-data.htm).

The OECD average tax-to-GDP ratio reached its highest level since the mid-1960s

In 2015, the average OECD tax-to-GDP ratio reached a new record level. The average tax-to-GDP ratio (based on preliminary data for 32 countries) rose by 0.1 percentage points compared to 2014, reaching 34.3%. This continued the trend of steady increases in tax levels in the period that followed the financial crisis, during which average tax revenues as a share of GDP in OECD countries fell to a low of 32.4% in 2009. Looking at longer term trends, the OECD average tax-to-GDP ratio in 2015 reached its highest level ever recorded since the OECD started collecting tax revenue data in the mid-1960s (Figure 2.3).

Following the crisis, the rise in tax revenues across OECD countries was in part the result of active fiscal consolidation measures. In addition to economic fluctuations which have effects on tax bases through changes in levels of employment, sales of goods and services and corporate profits, tax revenues are affected by changes in tax policy. In the years that followed the crisis, the adoption of tax reforms aimed at strengthening public finances was one of the factors accounting for the increase in tax revenues. Indeed, fiscal consolidation was the main driver of tax reforms across OECD countries after the crisis up until 2015 (OECD, 2016b). Looking at both the revenue and spending sides confirms governments' efforts to narrow budget deficits between 2010 and 2015: in almost all countries, tax increases were either accompanied by cuts in public spending or were greater than increases in government spending (Figure 2.4).

Figure 2.3. **Average tax-to-GDP ratio in the OECD, evolution until 2015**

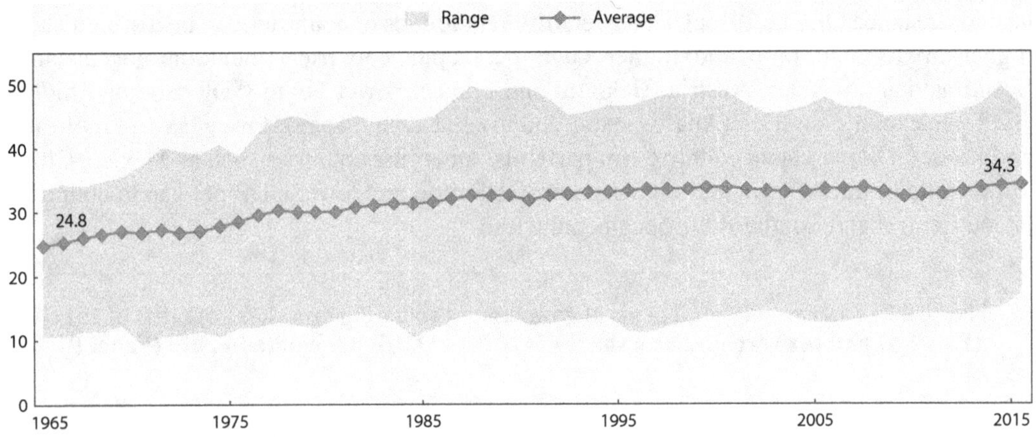

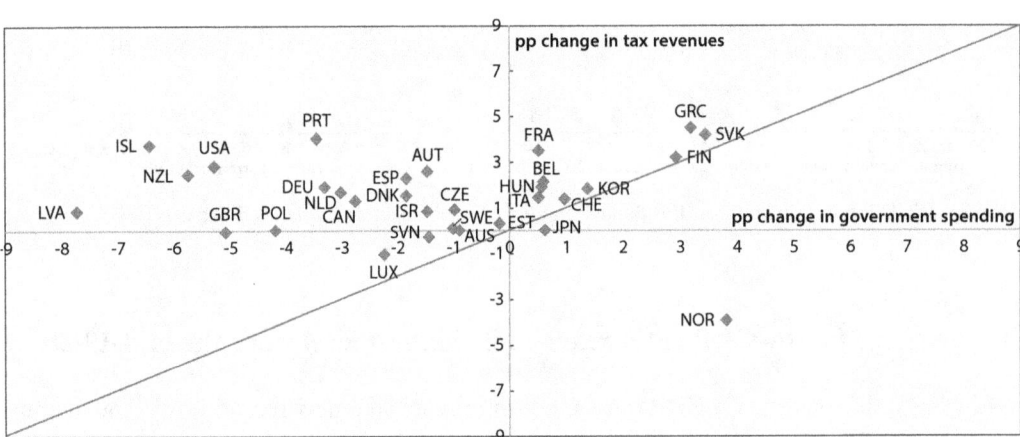

Note: The average tax-to-GDP ratio for 2015 is based on preliminary data for 32 countries.

Source: OECD Revenue Statistics, http://dx.doi.org/10.1787/data-00262-en.

Figure 2.4. **Percentage point changes in tax revenues and government spending as a share of GDP between 2010 and 2015**

Source: OECD Economic Outlook 100 database and Regional Revenue Statistics databases (www.oecd.org/tax/tax-policy/revenue-statistics-comparable-tax-revenue-data.htm).

Most countries saw their tax-to-GDP ratios increase between 2014 and 2015

Most countries experienced increases in their tax-to-GDP ratios between 2014 and 2015. Twenty-five of the 32 countries for which 2015 tax revenue data is available experienced an increase in their tax-to-GDP ratio between 2014 and 2015, reflecting the fact that tax revenues increased at a faster rate than GDP (except in Greece where GDP growth was negative). The largest tax-to-GDP ratio increase between 2014 and 2015 was recorded in Mexico (2.3 percentage points), which has the lowest tax-to-GDP ratio in the OECD. The special tax on production and services (*impuesto especial sobre produccion y servicios*) was the tax which recorded the largest revenue increase, in particular thanks to greater revenues collected from gasoline and diesel consumption. Revenue increases were also recorded in CIT and PIT, in part reflecting the impact of Mexico's comprehensive tax reform in 2014. Other countries which experienced substantial revenue increases (greater than one percentage point) included Turkey, Estonia, Greece, Hungary and the Slovak Republic. In most of these countries, revenue increases were relatively balanced across the major categories of taxes (Figure 2.5).

A minority of countries saw their tax-to-GDP ratio fall between 2014 and 2015, but decreases were particularly sharp in some countries. Only seven countries experienced a decrease in their tax-to-GDP ratios in 2015 relative to 2014. The decrease was sharpest in Ireland, where exceptional nominal GDP growth of over 30% led to a decrease of tax-to-GDP levels of over 5 percentage points. Although the nominal amount of tax revenues increased by 8.8% from 2014 to 2015, the higher GDP growth during this period caused the tax-to-GDP ratio to fall sharply. Interestingly, Ireland experienced a decline in revenues as a share of GDP in all major categories of taxes, except in corporate tax revenues, which increased slightly between 2014 and 2015 (Figure 2.5). The tax-to-GDP ratio in Denmark decreased by 3.0 percentage points, driven by a correction from unusually high income tax revenues in 2014. Decreases of more than one percentage point were also recorded in Iceland and Luxembourg, where growth rates were relatively high, respectively close to 10% and 7% between 2014 and 2015. In Norway, the sharp drop in CIT revenues was mainly due to the decline in earnings in the oil sector. Finally, it is worth noting that Norway and Denmark were the only two countries which experienced a drop in tax revenues in absolute value (measured in national currency).

Figure 2.5. **Percentage point changes in tax-to-GDP ratios by country between 2014 and 2015**

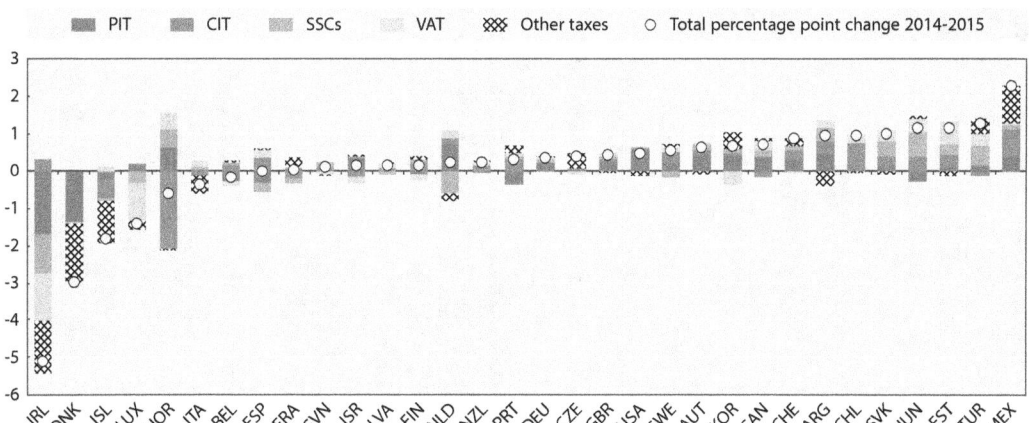

Note: No 2015 data for Australia, Japan, Poland and South Africa. No data for Greece.

Source: Regional Revenue Statistics databases (www.oecd.org/tax/tax-policy/revenue-statistics-comparable-tax-revenue-data.htm)?

Trends over a longer period of time show that the vast majority of OECD countries experienced increases in their tax-to-GDP ratios. Only four OECD countries (Norway, Ireland, Luxembourg and Slovenia) reported lower tax-to-GDP ratios in 2015 than in 2010 (Figure 2.6). All the other countries experienced increases ranging from 0.02 to 4.5 percentage points. Generally, countries with high public debts after the crisis experienced greater increases in their tax-to-GDP ratios although there were important exceptions (Figure 2.7, Panel A). There was also a negative correlation between total tax revenues as a share of GDP in 2010 and the percentage change in tax revenues between 2010 and 2015, suggesting a convergence trend in tax-to-GDP ratios across countries (Figure 2.7, Panel B). However, more work is needed to better understand convergence patterns in tax-to-GDP ratios across countries.

Figure 2.6. **Percentage point changes in tax-to-GDP ratios by country between 2010 and 2015**

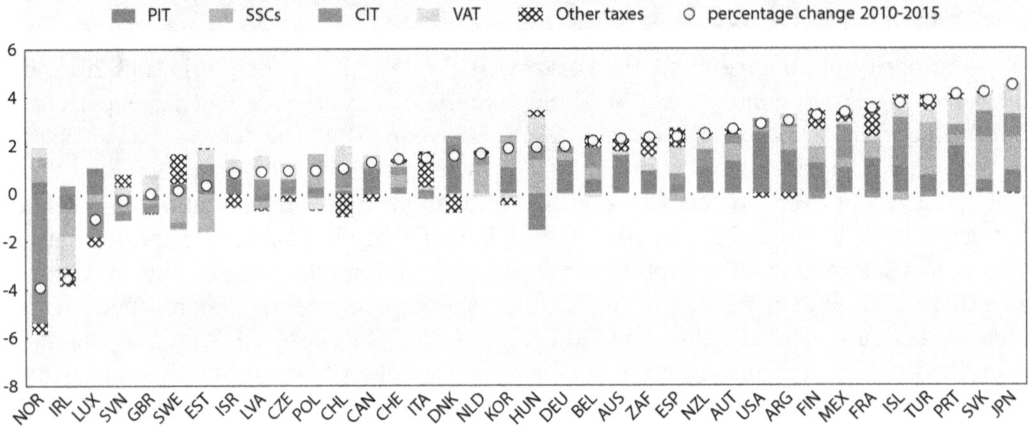

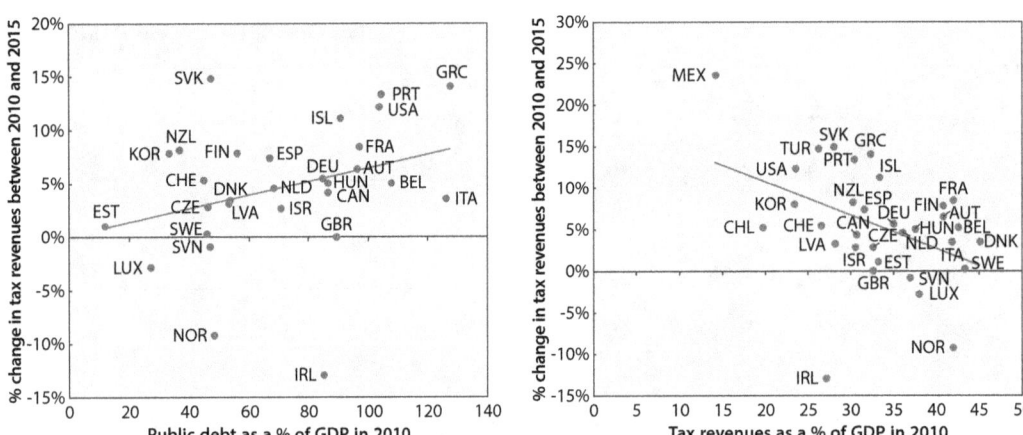

Note: No data for Greece; 2014 data used for Australia, Japan, Poland and South Africa.

Source: Regional Revenue Statistics databases (www.oecd.org/tax/tax-policy/revenue-statistics-comparable-tax-revenue-data.htm).

Figure 2.7. **Tax revenue increases between 2010 and 2015 and public debt (Panel A) and tax revenue levels in 2010 (Panel B)**

Source: OECD Economic Outlook 100 database and OECD Revenue Statistics, http://dx.doi.org/10.1787/data-00262-en.

In many countries, revenue increases between 2010 and 2015 reflected increases in revenues from PIT, SSCs and VAT. Large revenue increases in PIT drove total tax revenue increases in Argentina, Australia, Austria, Canada, Denmark, Germany, Portugal and the United States. Total tax revenue increases largely reflect SSC revenue increases in Hungary, Korea, the Netherlands, Poland and Turkey. In Chile, the Czech Republic, Hungary, Latvia and Spain, VAT revenues were a major driver of total tax revenue increases. CIT revenues, on the other, explained more than half of the revenue increases in Iceland and Mexico and were the main factor behind the tax revenue decrease in Norway (Figure 2.6).

The structure of tax revenues continued to shift towards labour and consumption taxes

The OECD's average tax mix is dominated by SSCs, PIT and VAT. The tax mix – or composition of total tax revenues – is an important indicator given that different taxes have different economic and distributional effects (OECD, 2010; Brys et al., 2016). SSCs, PIT and VAT each accounted for, on average, between a fifth and a quarter of total tax revenues in OECD countries in 2014.[1] On the other hand, corporate and property tax revenues accounted for smaller shares of total tax revenues, respectively making up 8.8% and 5.6% of the OECD's average tax mix in 2014.

In recent years, tax revenues in OECD countries have shifted towards greater shares of labour taxes and VAT. Revenues from income taxes reached 33.7% of total tax revenues in 2014. Within this category, the share of PIT in total tax revenues continued to increase following the crisis, reaching 24% of total tax revenues in 2014, while the share of CIT revenues in total taxation did not bounce back to pre-crisis levels, remaining below 9% of total tax revenues in 2014, compared to 11.2% in 2007, shifting more of the income tax burden towards households. With regard to SSCs, their share in total tax revenues increased markedly after the crisis, from 24.7% in 2007 to 26.8% in 2009 but then decreased slowly to just over 26% of total tax revenues on average in 2014. The OECD average share of property taxes in total taxation remained stable. Finally, regarding consumption taxes, the share of revenues from VAT has been increasing since 2007 and reached just over 20% in 2014, while revenues from taxes on specific goods and services, notably excises, remained close to their 2007 level, at 12.5% of total tax revenues, but decreased compared to their average share of 13.7% of total tax revenues in the OECD in 2000 (Figure 2.8).

Figure 2.8. **Evolution of the average tax mix in the OECD, % of total tax revenues**

Source: OECD Revenue Statistics, http://dx.doi.org/10.1787/data-00262-en.

Nevertheless, the structure of total tax revenues varies across countries. Income taxes, including both PIT and CIT, account for the largest source of tax revenues in 16 OECD countries. In Denmark, Australia, New Zealand and the United States, PIT accounts for 40% or more of total tax revenues, which is explained by the fact that Denmark, Australia and New Zealand do not collect SSCs and partly explained by the comparatively small share of revenues from consumption taxes in the United States. In a number of countries, including Central European and large Western European countries, SSCs are the primary source of tax revenues. There is a third group of OECD countries which collect most of their tax revenues from consumption taxes (Figure 2.9). Consumption taxes are also the main source of tax revenues in Argentina and play an important role in South Africa where they are the second largest source of tax revenues after income taxes, including both PIT and CIT.

Figure 2.9. **Tax revenue mixes by country in 2014, % of total tax revenues**

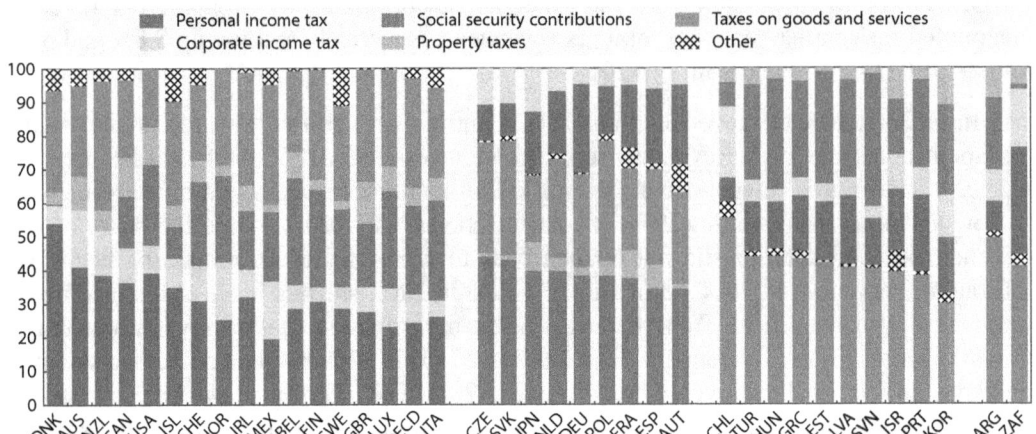

Source: Regional Revenue Statistics databases (www.oecd.org/tax/tax-policy/revenue-statistics-comparable-tax-revenue-data.htm).

Recent shifts in tax mixes have been driven by a combination of factors. As mentioned earlier, trends in tax revenues result from both changes in macroeconomic variables such as consumption, employment or profits, and from policy choices. The shift in tax revenues towards greater shares of PIT, SSCs and VAT was partly the result of post-crisis tax reforms which, to a large extent, focused on increasing those taxes (OECD, 2016b). For instance, standard VAT rates in the OECD reached a record level of 19.2% on average in 2015 and ten OECD countries now have a standard VAT rate above 22%, against only four in 2008. Labour taxes were also raised, with the OECD average tax wedge on labour income increasing in the years following the crisis, although this trend started reversing in 2013. Recent shifts in the tax mix also reflect the fact that revenues from some taxes, in particular from CIT, tend to be more responsive to economic fluctuations and business cycles than revenues from other taxes (Leblanc et al., 2013).

Note

1. 2014 is the latest year for which OECD average tax mix data is available.

References

Brys, B., Perret, S., Thomas, A. and P. O'Reilly (2016), "Tax Design for Inclusive Economic Growth", *OECD Taxation Working Papers*, No. 26, OECD Publishing, Paris, http://dx.doi.org/10.1787/5jlv74ggk0g7-en.

LeBlanc, P., S. Matthews and K. Mellbye (2013), "The Tax Policy Landscape Five Years after the Crisis", *OECD Taxation Working Papers*, No. 17, OECD Publishing, Paris, http://dx.doi.org/10.1787/5k40l4dxk0hk-en.

OECD (2016), *Revenue Statistics 2016*, OECD Publishing, Paris, http://dx.doi.org/10.1787/rev_stats-2016-en-fr.

OECD (2016b), *Tax Policy Reforms in the OECD 2016*, OECD Publishing, Paris, http://dx.doi.org/10.1787/9789264260399-en.

OECD (2016f), *Revenue Statistics in Asian Countries 2016: Trends in Indonesia, Japan, Korea, Malaysia, the Philippines and Singapore*, OECD Publishing, Paris, http://dx.doi.org/10.1787/9789264266483-en.

OECD (2010), *Tax Policy Reform and Economic Growth*, OECD Publishing, Paris, http://dx.doi.org/10.1787/9789264091085-en.

Chapter 3

Tax policy reforms in 2016

This chapter provides an overview of the tax reforms that were introduced in 2016 in OECD countries, Argentina and South Africa. It identifies the most significant tax reforms that were implemented, legislated or announced during calendar year 2016 as well as common tax policy trends across groups of countries. It starts with a summary of tax reforms across all countries and a brief overview of the countries that introduced the most comprehensive tax reforms in 2016. It then looks at trends in each category of tax separately, including personal income taxes and social security contributions, corporate income taxes, VAT/GST and excise duties, environmentally related taxes and property taxes.

The statistical data for Israel are supplied by and under the responsibility of the relevant Israeli authorities. The use of such data by the OECD is without prejudice to the status of the Golan Heights, East Jerusalem and Israeli settlements in the West Bank under the terms of international law.

This chapter provides an overview of the tax reforms that were introduced in 2016 in OECD countries, Argentina and South Africa. It identifies the most significant tax reforms that were implemented, legislated or announced during calendar year 2016 as well as common tax policy trends across groups of countries. It starts with a summary of tax reforms across all countries and a brief overview of the countries that introduced the most comprehensive tax reforms in 2016. It then looks at trends in each category of tax separately including personal income taxes and social security contributions, corporate income taxes and other corporate taxes, VAT/GST and excise duties, environmentally related taxes and property taxes.

The discussion in this chapter is primarily based on countries' responses to the 2017 Annual Tax Policy Reform Questionnaire which requested information on the tax reforms that were implemented, legislated or announced between 1 January and 31 December 2016. The questionnaire asked responding countries to describe the reforms as well as to provide details on their expected revenue effects and other relevant information, including the rationale for the measures (see Box 3.1).

Box 3.1. The OECD Annual Tax Policy Reform Questionnaire

At the Working Party No.2 on Tax Policy Analysis and Tax Statistics (WP2) meeting in November 2009, delegates from member countries agreed to start collecting more systematic information on the main tax measures adopted in each country. The motivation for this proposal was to provide consistent and comparative information on tax reforms to inform policy discussions in OECD countries.

At the November 2010 WP2 meeting, the following criteria were agreed for deciding whether a tax policy measure was sufficiently substantial to be reported in the questionnaire:

- A significant change in a tax rate;
- A change in the tax base that is expected to change revenue from that base by more than 5% or 0.1% of GDP; and
- A politically important systemic reform.

Any central or sub-central tax policy measure that was implemented, legislated or announced in the previous calendar year which meets at least one of the criteria listed above must be reported in the questionnaire.

For each reform, the questionnaire requests information on the type of tax; the dates of entry into force, legislation or announcement; the direction of the rate and/or base change; and a detailed description of the reform. The questionnaire also asks for the rationale behind the reform and estimates of the revenue effects of the tax measures.

The 2016 questionnaire was significantly streamlined compared to previous versions. In particular, many of the fields in the questionnaire were converted into drop-down menus. The objective was to facilitate data input by member country delegates as well as data use and analysis by the OECD Secretariat.

Two additional changes were introduced in the 2017 questionnaire: a joint questionnaire was developed for countries that are members of both the OECD and the European Union (EU); the questionnaire was also sent to two non-OECD G20 countries – Argentina and South Africa – in an effort to broaden the scope of the report beyond the OECD membership.

Reforms were generally growth oriented

The tax reforms that were introduced in 2016 can be viewed to a large extent as a response to low growth and were in part enabled by improvements in public budgets in many countries. As mentioned in Chapter 1, global growth was around 3% in 2016, its slowest annual pace since 2009 and well below the average of around 4% seen in the two decades before the crisis. To stimulate growth, numerous reforms sought to make countries more attractive to investment, in particular through reductions in CIT rates. Fiscal stimulus was also provided to individuals through reductions in PIT and, to a lesser extent, in SSCs. These reforms were enabled partly by improvements in public finances as public debts stabilised and budget deficits narrowed in many countries (Chapter 1).

Enhancing fairness was another important driver of tax reforms. As discussed in Chapter 1, inequality has generally increased in the OECD. While the recovery since 2010 improved average disposable incomes, more rapid growth of top incomes and weaker improvement at the bottom and the middle increased inequality. In this context, the numerous PIT cuts targeted at low and middle-income earners have often been driven by a desire to enhance fairness in addition to supporting growth. These reforms should continue raising the progressivity of PIT rate schedules at low income levels in many countries, but they might not raise the overall redistributive effect of PITs (see section 3.1).

Finally, deterring harmful consumption and behaviours motivated a number of reforms. Many reforms related to excise duties and environmentally related taxes, in particular, aimed at deterring harmful behaviours and consumption through tax increases. Another example has been the introduction of taxes on immovable property in a few countries to prevent the development of housing market bubbles. It should be mentioned, however, that some types of harmful behaviours remain far less taxed than others. In the area of

Table 3.1. **Expected revenue effects of the tax reforms implemented, legislated or announced in 2016**

Revenue ⇩		Revenue ⇧
ARG AUS AUT BEL CZE DEU EST FIN GBR HUN IRL ISL ISR LUX MEX NLD PRT SVN	Personal income tax	CAN CHE DNK GRC ITA KOR NOR SWE
BEL CHE DEU EST HUN ISL LUX ITA POL	SSCs and payroll taxes	ESP FIN GBR GRC SVK SWE
ARG AUT GBR HUN ISL ISR LUX MEX NZL POL PRT SVK TUR	Corporate income tax	CHL ESP (EST) KOR LVA SVN SWE ZAF
ARG FIN HUN JPN MEX PRT SWE TUR	Value-added tax	AUS AUT BEL CAN CZE ESP GBR GRC ITA LVA NOR NZL POL
	Non-energy excise duties	ARG AUS BEL ESP EST (GBR) GRC HUN IRL ISL LUX LVA NLD NZL PRT SVK SVN SWE ZAF
DNK GBR	Environmentally related taxes	BEL CAN EST FIN FRA GRC HUN ISL KOR LVA NLD NOR POL SWE
DNK IRL ITA NLD NOR TUR	Property taxes	AUT BEL CHL DEU GBR FIN FRA ISR LUX ZAF

Note: Countries in brackets have only announced reforms with positive or negative revenue effects. The table does not take into account reforms that were introduced before 2016 and which may have had revenue effects in 2016. It only takes into account the reforms that were implemented, legislated or announced in 2016. Countries for which revenue effects are unclear are omitted from this table.
Source: OECD Annual Tax Policy Reform Questionnaire.

environmentally related taxes, for instance, taxes on transport fuels, which are considerably higher than in other sectors continued to be increased in many countries, while fuels in other sectors which also cause considerable harm for the environment and human health often remain taxed at very low rates.

Countries generally expect negative revenue effects from PIT and CIT reforms and revenue increases from consumption, property and environmentally related taxes. Table 3.1 summarises the revenue effects of the tax policy measures that were reported in the 2017 Annual Tax Policy Reform Questionnaire. These measures include (1) the reforms that entered into force in 2016; (2) the reforms that were legislated in 2016, which for the most part entered into force in 2017; and (3) the reforms that were announced in 2016 and which might come into effect in 2017 or later. This table is not intended to provide a precise estimation of the revenue effects of reforms but gives an idea of the broad tax revenue shifts that can be expected. The table suggests that while most CIT and PIT reforms are expected to have negative effects on revenues, revenue increases are expected in many countries from VAT, excise duties, property taxes and environmentally related taxes which are considered less detrimental to economic growth than direct taxes (OECD, 2010).

Top tax reformers were predominantly EU countries

From a country perspective, top tax reformers in 2016 were almost all EU countries, with Austria, Belgium, Greece, Hungary, Luxembourg, the Netherlands and Norway identified as the countries that implemented or legislated the most comprehensive tax reforms in 2016. Comprehensive tax reforms are defined in this report as reforms that cover a wide number of tax areas and are generally presented by governments as reform packages with far-reaching objectives.

In line with overall trends, comprehensive tax reforms were generally growth oriented. With the exception of Greece, which continued to introduce direct and indirect tax reforms in 2016 to meet its fiscal targets under its third bailout programme, tax reforms were generally aimed at supporting growth, through fiscal stimulus for individuals or businesses or through pro-growth tax shifts. In Austria, Belgium and the Netherlands, comprehensive tax reforms came into force in 2016 with the main objective of reducing taxes on labour income. Norway introduced a significant package of measures designed to shift the tax burden away from corporate income towards tax bases that are less detrimental to growth and less sensitive to profit shifting, with some measures becoming effective in 2016 and others in 2017. Finally, Hungary and Luxembourg enacted comprehensive reforms in 2016 which entered into force in 2017. Hungary's package of substantial tax cuts aims at enhancing the economy's competitiveness while Luxembourg combined measures aimed among other objectives at enhancing its investment climate and increasing fairness.

Reflecting the fact that reforms were generally growth oriented, the countries that introduced comprehensive reforms generally expect negative short-term revenue effects. While positive revenue effects are anticipated in Greece, all the other countries reported negative revenue effects for 2016 or 2017 including Austria (slightly below EUR 2 billion for 2016), Belgium (around EUR 2.4 billion for 2016), the Netherlands (above EUR 4 billion for 2016[1]), Hungary (around EUR 1.7 billion for 2017[2]), Luxembourg (EUR 373 million in 2017) and Norway (around EUR 550 million in 2016 and EUR 225 million in 2017[3]). These revenue estimations also show that comprehensive labour tax reforms are expected to be much more costly than comprehensive corporate tax reforms.

The fiscal sustainability of these reform packages depends on a number of factors including the adoption of spending-side measures and countries' overall budget balances, the introduction of non-tax measures that will have an impact on tax revenues (e.g. positive impact on tax revenues of the minimum wage increase in Hungary), and the longer run growth effects of tax reforms. As shown in Figure 3.1, the countries that introduced fiscal stimulus reforms are in different fiscal positions. While Norway and Luxembourg recorded budget surpluses in 2015, Austria, Hungary and the Netherlands had moderate budget deficits and Belgium's deficit was above 2% of GDP.

Figure 3.1. **Budget balances as a share of GDP in countries that introduced fiscal stimulus packages in 2016**

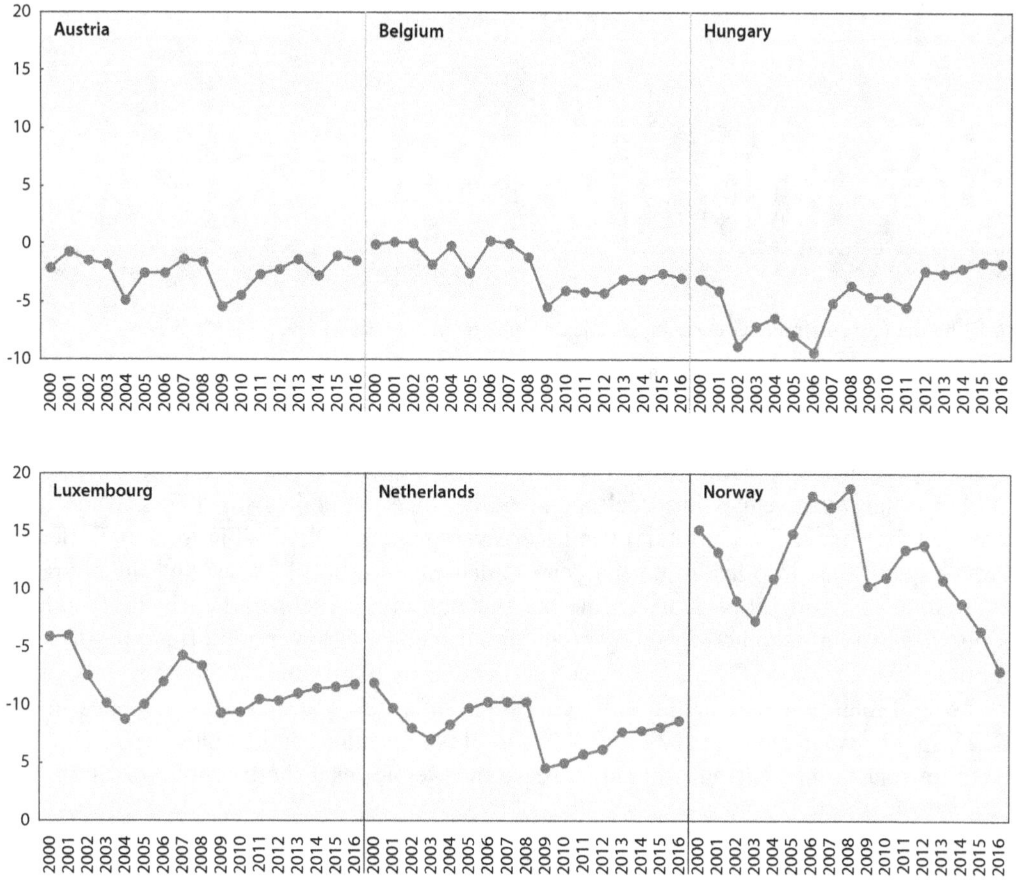

Source: OECD Economic Outlook 100 database.

3.1. Personal income tax and social security contributions

Labour taxes are the most important source of tax revenues in OECD countries on average

PIT and SSCs account for over half of total tax revenues on average in OECD countries and for a third of revenues in Argentina and South Africa. On average, PIT accounted for 24% of total tax revenues in OECD countries in 2014, while SSCs accounted for more than 26% of total tax revenues. In Austria, Germany, the United States and Sweden, PIT, SSCs and payroll taxes together accounted for more than 60% of total tax revenues in 2015. Even in countries where the reliance on those taxes is comparatively low, they still represent a significant share of revenues. In New Zealand, Israel and Mexico, PIT, SSCs and payroll taxes accounted for around 40% of total tax revenues in 2015 and about a third of total tax revenues came from those taxes in Argentina and South Africa. Chile is an exception, as the country raised only 14% of its total tax revenues through PIT and SSCs in 2015 (Figure 3.2).

Figure 3.2. **PIT, SSCs and payroll tax revenues as a share of total taxation by country in 2015**

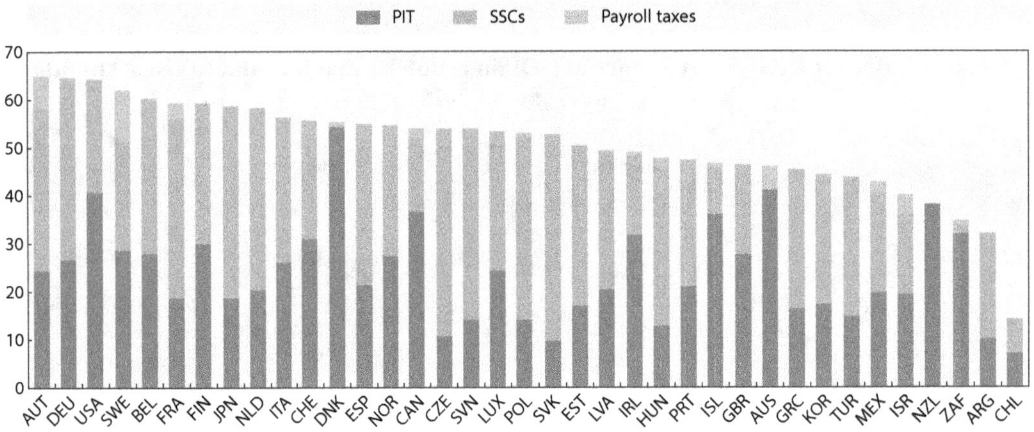

Note: 2014 data for Australia, Greece, Japan, Mexico, Poland and South Africa.

Source: Regional Revenue Statistics databases (www.oecd.org/tax/tax-policy/revenue-statistics-comparable-tax-revenue-data.htm).

However, the composition of labour tax revenues has evolved over time. The share of PIT in total tax revenues has declined steadily since the end of the 1970s, when they accounted for close to 32% of total revenues on average in the OECD (Figure 3.3). Different factors explain this drop including the general decrease in top PIT rates and the adoption in a number of countries of dual income tax systems in the 1980s and early 1990s which tax personal capital income separately from labour income at lower and often proportional tax rates. By contrast, SSC revenues have been gradually increasing. While they accounted for 17.6% of total revenues in 1965, they became the largest source of tax revenues in the OECD, split between employee SSCs (9.5% of total tax revenues) and employer SSCs (14.7% of total revenues). The average annual increase in revenues as a share of total taxation was

Figure 3.3. **PIT, SSCs and payroll tax revenues as a share of total taxation, OECD average, 1965-2014**

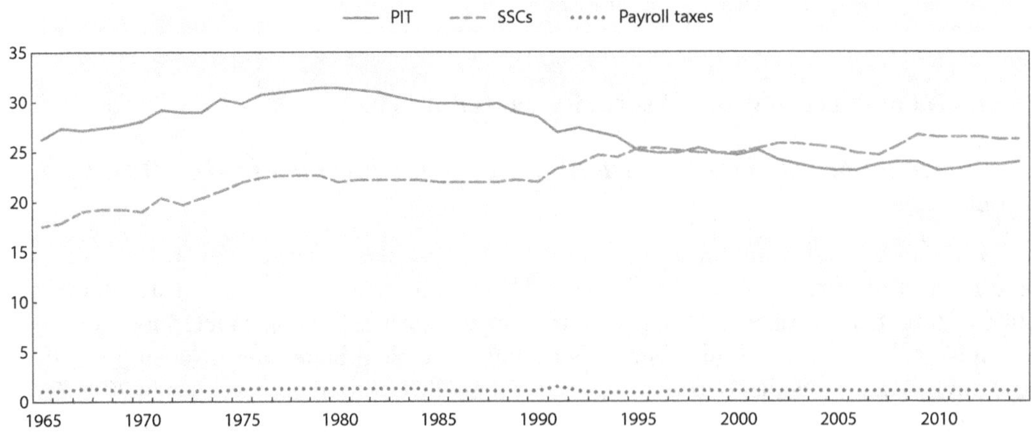

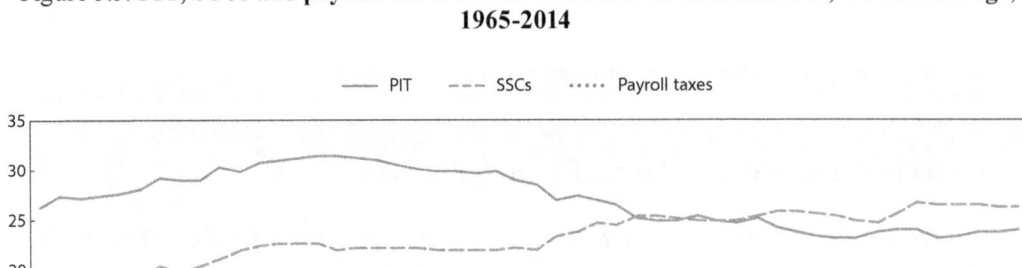

Source: OECD Revenue Statistics, http://dx.doi.org/10.1787/data-00262-en.

slightly higher for employee SSCs at 1.1% than for employer SSCs at 0.9% between 1965 and 2014. This trend has become clearer in recent years: the average annual revenue increase for employee SSCs was significantly higher at 0.7% compared to an average increase of employer SSCs revenues of 0.1% between 2000 and 2014.

Taxes on labour income declined on average between 2013 and 2016, after a series of post-crisis increases

In the years following the crisis, the average tax burden on labour income increased steadily in the OECD (OECD, 2017a and 2016b). Between 2009 and 2013, the OECD average tax wedge – or total tax payments on labour income as a percentage of labour costs – for single workers earning the average wage increased by one percentage point, from 35.2% to 36.2% (Figure 3.4). This was mainly for fiscal consolidation purposes (OECD, 2016a) and in stark contrast with the period from the early 2000s until the crisis during which the tax burden on labour income decreased substantially (Figure 3.4), in particular for families with children (see Figure 3.5). In the post-crisis period, tax wedges rose broadly on all family types, with a particular concentration on one-earner married couples with children. However, even though these average rates have risen since the crisis, tax wedges are still below where they were in the early 2000s.

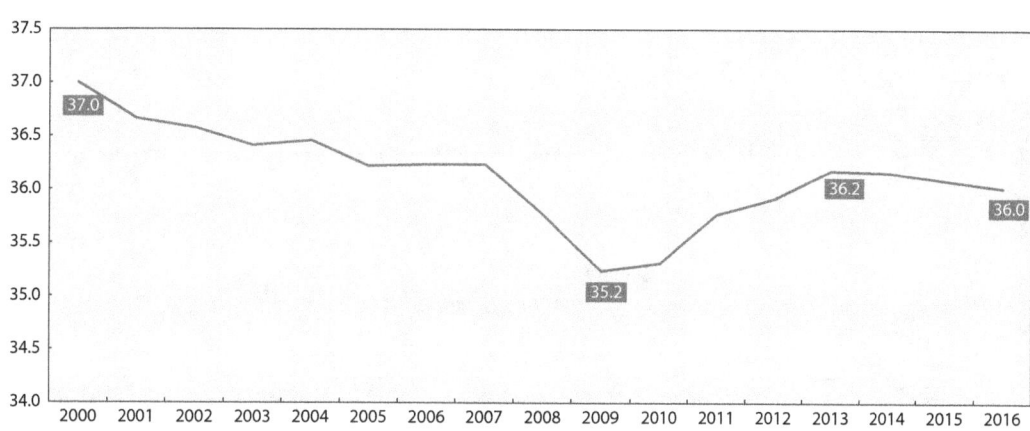

Figure 3.4. **Evolution of the average tax wedge in the OECD between 2000 and 2016**

Average tax wedge for a single person earning 100% of the average wage

Source: OECD Taxing Wages Database, http://dx.doi.org/10.1787/data-00265-en.

Since 2013, the average tax burden on labour income in the OECD has been decreasing slowly (OECD, 2017a and 2016b). After three years of small consecutive declines, the tax wedge on the income of the average worker in the OECD reached 36.0% in 2016. Despite an overall declining trend, between 2015 and 2016, the tax wedge actually increased slightly in 20 of the 35 OECD countries (Figure 3.6). The overall decrease in the average tax wedge is partly explained by significant reforms in some countries, in particular Austria and Belgium, which aimed at reducing taxes on labour income to support growth and employment (see Chapter 1 and OECD, 2016a). Austria introduced several PIT cuts which lowered the average tax wedge by about 2.5 percentage points. Belgium reduced employer and self-employed SSCs, reduced PIT rates and introduced an increase in the "work bonus", resulting in a decrease in the average tax wedge of about 1.5 percentage points. In Greece, on the other hand, the tax wedge increased by more than 1 percentage point as a result of increases in PIT and SSCs.

Figure 3.5. **Changes in labour income tax wedges in OECD countries before and after the financial crisis by family type**

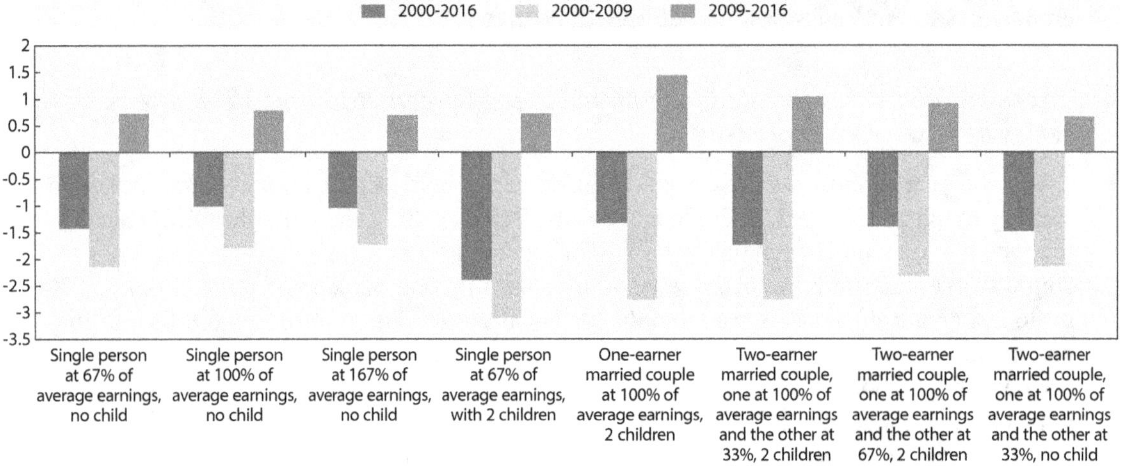

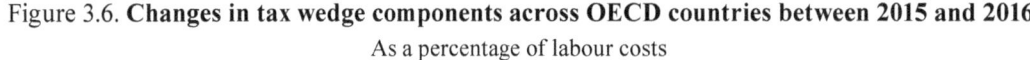

Source: OECD Taxing Wages Database, http://dx.doi.org/10.1787/data-00265-en.

Figure 3.6. **Changes in tax wedge components across OECD countries between 2015 and 2016**
As a percentage of labour costs

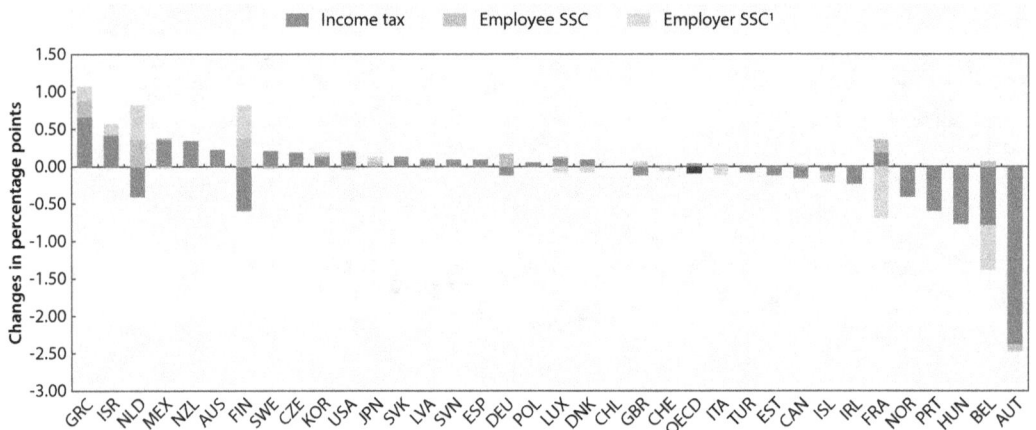

Note: Single individual without children at the average wage level. 1. Includes payroll taxes where applicable.
Source: OECD Taxing Wages Database, http://dx.doi.org/10.1787/data-00265-en.

The average tax wedge decreased also for low-income workers between 2015 and 2016. Significant reductions were recorded not only in Austria and Belgium but also in the Netherlands and Hungary. The Netherlands reduced non-top PIT rates and expanded earned income tax credits and the tax credit for people combining work and childcare. The average tax wedge also decreased in Hungary by more than 0.5 percentage points. The overall decrease in the tax burden on low-income workers for the OECD on average was small, however, because of tax burden increases in a number of other countries. Tax burden increases on low-income workers were particularly high in Greece where the average tax wedge increased by about 1.5 percentage points and, to a smaller extent, in Israel. Greece introduced a wide range of measures that took effect in 2016, including higher SSCs and PIT base broadening measures, moving from a schedular to a comprehensive PIT by taxing labour remuneration, pensions and personal business income jointly instead of taxing these income categories under a separate rate schedule. Israel reduced its basic tax credit and increased employer SSCs resulting in an increase in the average tax wedge of about 0.5 percentage points.

The recently legislated tax measures suggest that PITs will continue to become more progressive at lower income levels but their overall redistributive impact might not increase. The reforms that were introduced in 2016 have generally lowered PIT rates and narrowed PIT bases, in particular for lower and middle-income earners. The recent trend towards greater statutory PIT rate progressivity at lower income levels seems therefore set to continue (Box 3.2). In addition, there were more countries increasing than decreasing their top PIT rate. However, most of the PIT reforms that were introduced in 2016 are expected to have negative revenue effects. Therefore, despite increases in their statutory progressivity, the overall redistributive impact of PITs might not necessarily increase because of the decline in expected PIT revenues.

> Box 3.2. **Changes in labour income tax progressivity**
>
> Statutory labour income tax progressivity has risen in recent years, but not on high-income taxpayers. Broader measures of progressivity suggest that the effectiveness of the personal income tax system in reducing inequality has declined. The left panel of the figure below shows that tax progressivity in statutory tax rates has increased at lower income levels as governments have strengthened incentives for these workers to participate in the labour market. However the right panel of the figure shows that statutory tax progressivity is lower – and has fallen – at higher income levels. Recent OECD research using household micro-data to measure progressivity in terms of taxes paid has found that progressivity across the OECD has been flat or slightly increasing since the mid-90s (Causa and Hermansen, forthcoming). At the same time, this research has found that there has been a slight decline in the size of personal income taxes, which has meant that the effectiveness of these taxes in inequality reduction overall has fallen over this period.
>
> **Personal income tax progressivity has increased at the lower end of the income distribution, and decreased at higher income levels**
>
> Personal income tax progressivity by income level and family type
>
>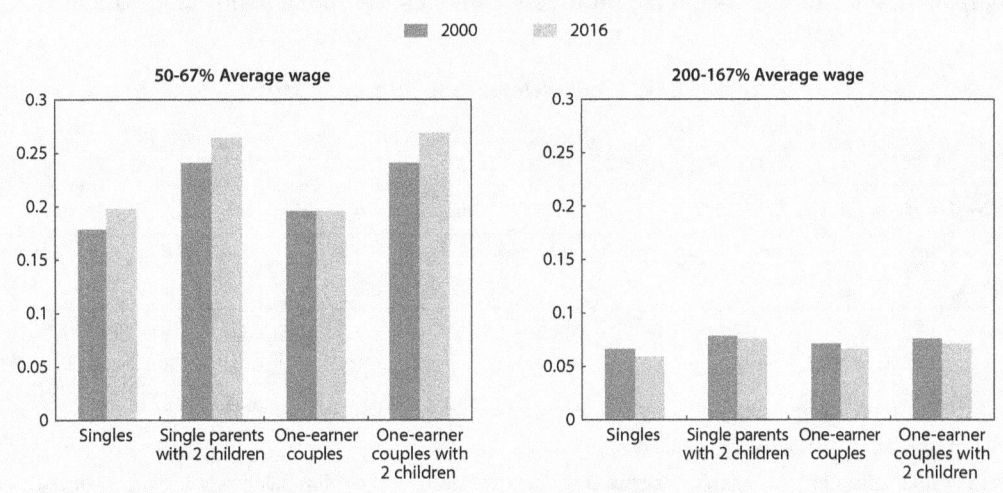
>
> *Source:* OECD calculations based on *Taxing Wages 2016* (OECD, 2016h).

While tax wedges – especially on low-wage earners – are expected to be further reduced in many countries as a consequence of recent PIT reforms, SSCs remain high in many countries. SSCs are typically levied at proportional rates and therefore hit low-income earners more strongly, pricing in particular lower-skilled workers out of the labour market. However, fundamental SSC reform is costly for public budgets and, despite attempts to lower SSCs in some countries where they were particularly high, they continue to be a major source of revenue across the OECD. In most countries (with the exception of Hungary which introduced a large cut in employer SSCs, Belgium which continues to phase in its SSC reform and Italy which introduced a two-year employer SSC cut for new permanent contracts), recent SSC reforms are not expected to significantly reduce tax burdens on labour income. To some extent, PIT reductions targeted at low-income earners can be viewed as partly offsetting the distortive impact of high SSCs in many OECD countries.

The majority of recent PIT reforms aim at reducing taxes on low and middle-income earners and are expected to lower PIT revenues

A majority of the PIT reforms that were introduced in 2016 are expected to lower PIT revenues. Many countries introduced PIT rate cuts and PIT base narrowing measures, with expected negative revenue effects. The 37 countries covered in the study reported a total of 77 PIT measures taking effect in 2016 and 85 PIT measures taking effect in 2017. Out of the 85 measures taking effect in 2017, 58 are expected to reduce PIT revenues, whereas 18 measures are expected to have a revenue raising effect. Two measures are expected to be revenue neutral while the revenue impacts of the other seven measures are uncertain or not available.

Regarding top PIT rates, there were more countries reporting tax rate increases than decreases. Four countries reported an increase in their top PIT rate taking effect in 2016 and five countries legislated top PIT rate increases entering into force 2017 or later (see Table 3.2). On the other hand, two countries reported a top PIT rate decrease in 2016 and four countries introduced a top PIT rate reduction coming into effect in 2017 or later. In Norway, the flat PIT rate on ordinary income was reduced from 27% to 25% in 2016 and then to 24% in 2017 to maintain the alignment with Norway's CIT rate (see section 3.2) as part of the country's dual income tax system. However, this PIT rate reduction was partly compensated by an increase in the progressive bracket tax which applies to gross income.

Table 3.2. **PIT rate reforms introduced in 2016**

	Rate ⇧		Rate ⇩	
Into effect in	2016	2017 or later	2016	2017 or later
Top PIT rate	AUT CAN GRC NOR	DNK ISR KOR LUX NOR	HUN NOR	FIN IRL* NOR PRT**
Non-top PIT rate(s)	GRC NOR	AUS DNK LUX NLD	AUS AUT BEL CAN FRA ISL NLD PRT	ARG BEL FIN FRA HUN IRL ISL ISR LUX PRT** SVN

* Ireland reduced the universal social charge.

** In Portugal, the PIT rates remain unchanged but the PIT surtax will be eliminated over the course of 2017.

Source: OECD Annual Tax Policy Reform Questionnaire.

The majority of PIT rate reforms in 2016 lowered tax rates on low and middle-income earners. Eight countries implemented non-top PIT rate reductions in 2016 while 11 countries reported similar reforms coming into effect in 2017. In some countries, these reforms were introduced with the objective of raising the net take-home pay of both low and middle-income earners. For instance, as part of its broader reform to shift taxation away from labour taxation, Belgium eliminated its 30% tax rate by integrating the 30% tax rate bracket into the 25% rate bracket, taking effect gradually in 2016 and 2018. Belgium also raised the income threshold of the 45% tax rate bracket, which will progressively be put into place in 2018 and 2019. In Ireland, the decrease in the Universal Social Charge came into effect in 2015 and 2016, raising the disposable income of low and middle-income earners. In Canada, Luxembourg and Slovenia, the tax rate cuts were specifically targeted at middle-income earners. Slovenia, for instance, introduced a new third tax bracket with a rate of 34% and lowered the PIT rate of the fourth tax bracket from 41% to 39%.

In some countries, the increase in the top PIT rate was accompanied by decreases in non-top PIT rates, increasing the progressivity of PIT rate schedules. In Austria, the existing three tax brackets were replaced by a schedule of six tax brackets, leading to a general reduction in PIT rates, except for top earners who are now subject to a new top marginal PIT rate of 55%. In Canada, the federal marginal tax rate on incomes between CAD 45 000 and 90 000 was lowered from 22% to 20.5%, while a new high income bracket was created for incomes over CAD 200 000 to be taxed at 33%. In Luxembourg, the PIT rate schedule was significantly revised, lowering tax rates on middle-income earners and introducing two new marginal PIT rates for the highest incomes. The top marginal rate that applies to taxable income above EUR 200 000 is now 42%. Israel reduced the tax rates that apply to low and middle incomes while it increased the surtax on all types of income from 2% to 3%. In Finland, on the other hand, the highest and the lowest central government PIT rates are being lowered jointly as part of a general tax cut on earned income to boost economic growth.

A vast majority of PIT measures have narrowed PIT bases

Many countries continued to narrow their PIT bases. Out of a total of 61 PIT base measures coming into effect in 2017 or later, 49 reforms narrowed tax bases (see Table 3.3). A much smaller number of countries have adopted measures broadening their PIT base; only 12 base broadening measures were reported as coming into effect in 2017 or later. This follows the pattern of the measures that took effect in 2016: 38 measures narrowed PIT bases while 21 measures broadened them.

A number of countries increased the generosity of their basic PIT provisions. For instance, increases in basic allowances, zero-rate bands or general tax credits were introduced in Argentina, Belgium, Germany, Norway, the Netherlands and the United Kingdom. In Estonia, as of 2018, the tax free allowance will be raised from EUR 180 to EUR 500 a month but will start diminishing from incomes of EUR 1 200 per month to zero for monthly incomes above EUR 2 100. In parallel, the tax-free allowance for pensions will be eliminated as of 2018 and the annual refunds to low-paid employees were abolished as of 2017.

A number of countries have narrowed their PIT bases with reforms targeted at families with children or home carers. Australia introduced a tax deduction for the contribution on behalf of a spouse to their superannuation fund; Germany increased its basic allowances for children and child benefits; Ireland increased the home carer tax credit; and Luxembourg increased the existing tax credit for single parents and tax allowances for expenses for children not residing with their parents. This trend is aligned with the measures that took effect in 2016, when seven countries expanded their provisions aimed at households with children and other dependents. Overall, these reforms stand in sharp contrast with the reforms implemented after the financial crisis, where households with children saw their income tax burdens rise more than families without children (see Figure 3.5).

Table 3.3. **PIT base reforms introduced in 2016**

	Base ⇧		Base ⇩	
Into effect in	2016	2017 or later	2016	2017 or later
Personal allowances, credits, tax brackets	AUS CAN FIN GBR GRC NLD SWE	AUS LUX SWE	ARG BEL DEU EST IRL ISL NLD SVK TUR	ARG DEU EST BEL FIN GBR IRL LUX LVA NOR NLD SVN
Targeted low-income/ EITCs	EST SWE	NLD	AUT FIN IRL NLD	FIN IRL LUX POL
Children & other dependents	EST		AUT CZE DEU HUN IRL NLD PRT	AUS (CZE) DEU HUN IRL LUX
Elderly & disabled			NLD SWE	NLD
Miscellaneous expenses & deductions	AUT CHE EST GRC SWE	AUS CAN (CZE) EST GBR LUX SWE	ARG AUT BEL FIN IRL MEX SWE TUR	BEL EST FIN HUN ISL LUX PRT SVK SWE

Notes: For the sake of simplicity, tax credits are treated as base provisions in the report.
Countries in brackets have only announced reforms.

Source: OECD Annual Tax Policy Reform Questionnaire.

Some countries introduced base narrowing measures specifically targeted at low-income earners. Many of those measures involved the expansion of earned income tax credits (EITCs), which have the dual goal of alleviating poverty and increasing incentives to work by targeting low-income workers and imposing some form of work-contingent eligibility rule. In 2016, Austria expanded its non-wastable tax credits for low-income earners. In Finland, the maximum annual amount of the EITC was raised from EUR 1 025 to EUR 1 260 in January 2016 and then to EUR 1 420 in January 2017. To address the disparity between employed and self-employed persons, Ireland introduced an EITC for self-employed workers as of 2016 with a maximum value of EUR 550, which was then raised to EUR 950 in 2017. In the Netherlands, there was a large increase in the maximum amount of the EITC from EUR 2 220 in 2015 to EUR 3 103 in 2016 as part of a comprehensive labour tax reform package and then a smaller increase to EUR 3 223 in 2017. In parallel, there was a decrease in the EITC for higher income earners. Finally, in Poland, the tax-free allowance was increased for low-income taxpayers and reduced for high-income earners to increase fairness.

Finland, Italy and Portugal narrowed their PIT base with a view to increasing entrepreneurship and innovation. Finland introduced a 5% tax deduction for entrepreneurs and the self-employed, and increased the tax deduction for work-related expenses. Portugal provided a deduction of up to 25% of all investments in start-ups, up to a limit of EUR 100 000 and 40% of the individuals' tax liability. In Italy, entrepreneurs may opt to be taxed under the new tax on entrepreneurial income (*imposta sul reddito d'impresa*, IRI). Under this new tax, personal business income which is reinvested will not be taxed under the regular PIT but will be taxed at a rate of 24%. The measure is aimed at reducing the tax burden on reinvested earnings for unincorporated businesses and at guaranteeing tax neutrality among different legal forms of business activity.

Tax provisions to attract highly skilled workers are being introduced. Some countries are increasingly competing against each other to attract high-income and highly-skilled taxpayers through their tax systems. Italy, for instance, approved a Finance Bill at the end of 2016 which foresees a four-year tax exemption on 90% of the remuneration for professors and researchers who move to Italy after having taught or researched outside of Italy for more than two years; a five-year tax exemption on 50% of the remuneration applies for managers and professionals who move back to Italy after having resided for at least five years outside of Italy. These measures existed before 2016 but have now been extended and will become effective in 2017.

In addition, tax competition to attract high-wealth individuals appears to be intensifying. Some countries focus on high-wealth individuals as an attempt to broaden their tax base and to stimulate entrepreneurship. Italy, for instance, allows individuals who become Italian residents after having resided for at least nine of the last 10 years outside of Italy to pay a yearly lump-sum substitute tax of EUR 100 000 (for a maximum of 15 years) on all foreign-source income instead of having to pay the regular PIT on this foreign-source income, in addition to the incentives for highly skilled workers mentioned above. Israel taxes only 75% of the income earned by certain foreign employees during the first three years of residence in Israel provided certain conditions are met. Portugal introduced a non-habitual residents (NHR) regime, which grants a special tax residency status if certain conditions are fulfilled. The regime provides for the total tax exemption on foreign source employment and capital income in Portugal, as long as the income has been taxed at source in accordance with the applicable tax treaty and does not have its source in a tax haven. In certain conditions, income derived from high-added value professions which has its source in Portugal may be liable to a 20% flat tax rate instead of being subject to the progressive PIT rate schedule.

On the other hand, some noticeable base broadening reforms were introduced. Sweden legislated four different base broadening measures. It introduced a limited upward adjustment of the threshold for state income tax, increased the limit for the deductibility of travel expenses, and adjusted the limits for both lower and higher income thresholds. Australia, Canada, Estonia, Luxembourg, the Netherlands and the United Kingdom have also introduced PIT base broadening measures coming into effect in 2017 or later. Australia implemented reforms to its residency rules to include seasonal workers as taxpayers; the United Kingdom broadened the PIT base by extending the measures to tackle the use of disguised remuneration of the self-employed; and Luxembourg has reformed its PIT rate schedule by decreasing the width of each tax bracket.

Some countries have limited or entirely removed tax expenditures which tend to be regressive. Reforms of this nature can be beneficial as they raise average tax rates without raising marginal rates (Brys et. al., 2016) and may help enhance the progressivity of tax systems at high income levels, which has declined on average in recent years (see Box 3.2). For example, Estonia limited mortgage interest deductibility, Luxembourg limited deductibility for consumption loans and Canada eliminated the education and textbook tax credit as well as the tax credits for children's fitness and arts. On the other hand, Luxembourg increased the mortgage interest deductibility on owner-occupied dwellings, and Sweden increased the tax deduction for household work and adjusted the limit of deductible travel expenses for individuals.

Despite some reform efforts, SSCs continue to weigh heavily on labour income

As discussed earlier, revenues from SSCs have been increasing over time across the OECD, although this trend seems to have come to a halt in recent years partly as a result of reforms which have sought to lower SSCs in countries where they were very high. Regarding recent SSC reforms, there are no clear trends in terms of revenue effects. Eleven countries reported reforms to SSCs coming into effect in 2016 while 13 countries legislated a total of 25 SSC measures taking effect in 2017 or later. Of the measures that take effect in 2017 or later, 13 are expected to have a revenue raising effect while 11 measures are expected to lower SSC revenues.

In 2016, several countries implemented reforms that reduced SSCs. Generally with a view to stimulating employment and competitiveness, Belgium, Estonia, Iceland, Luxembourg and Switzerland reduced employer SSC rates while Belgium and Italy narrowed the employer SSC base. Italy introduced a two-year employer SSC allowance with a maximum of EUR 3 250 for new employees hired on permanent contracts. Belgium, Estonia, Luxembourg, the Slovak Republic and Switzerland also lowered employee and/or self-employed SSCs. In contrast, Spain and Greece increased SSCs and/or broadened their base (Tables 3.4 and 3.5). Japan implemented reforms in both directions: they decreased the employee contribution rate for unemployment benefits from 0.5% to 0.4% and increased the employee pension insurance rate from 8.914% to 9.091%.

Table 3.4. **Reforms in SSC rates introduced in 2016**

	Rate ⇧		Rate ⇩	
Into effect in	2016	2017 or later	2016	2017 or later
Employers SSCs	GRC JPN	DEU GBR	BEL CHE EST ISL JPN LUX	(EST) FIN HUN
Employees SSCs	GRC JPN	DEU FIN	CHE EST JPN	LUX*
Self-employed	GRC		BEL CHE	HUN SWE
Payroll taxes				FRA HUN

Note: Countries in brackets have only announced reforms.
* In Luxembourg, the measure refers to the elimination of the temporary budget balancing tax.

Source: OECD Annual Tax Policy Reform Questionnaire.

No clear trend in SSC reforms can be distinguished from the reforms coming into effect in 2017. Finland, Germany and the United Kingdom have raised SSC rates while Greece, the Slovak Republic, Spain and the United Kingdom broadened their SSC bases; the Slovak Republic abolished its SSC upper ceiling and Spain increased its lower and upper SSC ceilings by respectively 8% and 3% (Tables 3.4 and 3.5). Germany increased employer and employee SSCs rates by 0.2 percentage points, and Finland increased employee SSCs while decreasing employer SSCs. The United Kingdom introduced significant SSC measures entering into force in 2017 and 2018: it removed SSC advantages for certain benefits in kind when provided through salary sacrifice arrangements, will apply SSCs to all termination payments over GBR 30 000 and grant entitlement to contributory benefits through the payment of SSCs to the self-employed. The most significant cuts in SSCs were implemented in Hungary which reduced the employer SSC and health contribution rates from 27% to 22% as of 2017, and further cuts – amounting to 8.5 percentage points in total – have been planned for subsequent years (2018-22), depending on wage developments.

Table 3.5. **Reforms in SSC bases introduced in 2016**

Into effect in	Base ⇧		Base ⇩	
	2016	2017 or later	2016	2017 or later
Employers SSCs	ESP JPN	ESP GBR SVK	BEL ITA	POL
Employees SSCs	ESP JPN	ESP GBR SVK	SVK	POL
Self-employed	ESP	ESP GRC		(FRA) GBR
Payroll taxes	SWE			

Note: Countries in brackets have only announced reforms.

Source: OECD Annual Tax Policy Reform Questionnaire.

Financing some social benefits through general taxation as opposed to SSCs could help ensure funding for welfare systems while lowering the tax burden on workers. High SSCs in particular on low incomes might price low-skilled workers out of the labour market, resulting in high levels of unemployment and low levels of labour market participation in particular amongst the most vulnerable groups of workers. In addition, structural changes in the economy as a result of digitalisation, automation and other trends are resulting in an increasing numbers of self-employed, temporary workers and workers with irregular working hours, which pay lower levels of SSCs. This trend presents new challenges not only for tax administrations but also for welfare systems financed by SSCs. Financing some social benefits through general taxation instead, in particular those for which assistance is not closely linked to the level of contributions made such as health benefits and family cash transfers, can help raise labour market participation, reduce labour market dualism, boost growth, and at the same time extend welfare support to a greater number of people.

Relatively few countries have reformed taxes on capital income at the individual level

Countries continue to strengthen their Exchange of Information relationships, allowing countries to tax capital income effectively and efficiently (Figure 3.7). The OECD Global Forum on Transparency and Exchange of Information for Tax Purposes, which is the continuation of a forum that was created in the early 2000s and restructured in 2009, is a multilateral framework open to both OECD and non-OECD countries to implement transparency and exchange of information for tax purposes. The Global Forum has developed two different international standards for the exchange of information for tax purposes: the Exchange of Information on Request (EOIR) and the Automatic Exchange of Information (AEOI). For the EOIR, countries undergo an evaluation known as peer review, which evaluates their compliance with the standard. For the purpose of AEOI, a Common Reporting Standard (CRS) has been developed that is implemented into domestic law of participating jurisdictions. Through both the EOIR and the AEOI, countries reduce the extent to which individuals and companies are able to use offshore accounts and structures to avoid and evade taxes. The introduction of the AEOI as well as the steady development of EOIR mark a step change in tax transparency, but there must be continued focus on the peer review process and on the development of the network of exchange of information agreements for these new systems to maximise their effectiveness (see Box 3.3).

Figure 3.7. **The growth in EOIR relationships created since 2009**
Bilateral Relationships and the Multilateral Convention on Mutual Administrative Assistance in Tax Matters (MAC)

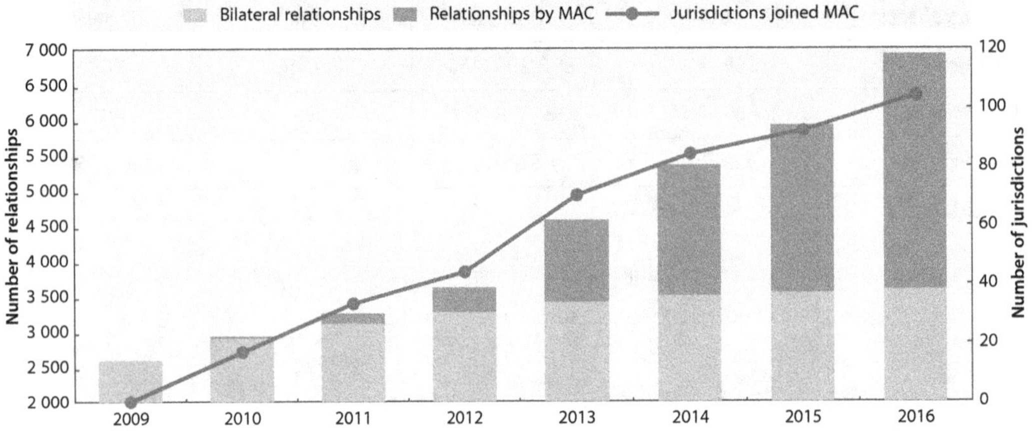

Source: Tax Transparency 2016: Report on Progress (Global Forum on Transparency and Exchange of Information for Tax Purposes, 2016).

Box 3.3. **The exchange of information on tax matters and tackling tax evasion**

The Global Forum now has over 140 members on an equal footing and is the premier international body for ensuring the implementation of exchange of information in the tax area. Exchange of information has been a key change in the international tax architecture in recent years with respect to the taxation of capital income. The Global Forum has pursued this work along two main lines; Exchange of Information on Request (EOIR) and Automatic Exchange of Information (AEOI).

EOIR has long been a component of tax treaties; however, it has greatly expanded through the increased use of the International Standard of Exchange of Information on Request (Global Forum on Transparency and Exchange of Information for Tax Purposes, 2016). There are currently almost 7000 EOIR relationships (see Figure 3.7).

Ninety-eight countries have committed to exchange information automatically. There are currently 1300 bilateral exchange relationships activated based on the OECD's Multilateral Convention on Mutual Administrative Assistance in Tax Matters (MAC), bilateral information exchange agreements and EU directives on information exchange. This means that AEOI does not yet have the same coverage as EOIR, though this should change with time.

EOIR appears to have had an impact; initial statistical studies suggest that taxpayer information exchange agreements do reduce tax evasion through the use of offshore havens (Braun and Weichenrieder, 2015; Hanlon et al., 2015). However, studies also show that in response to the signing of agreements, taxpayers seeking to avoid tax may shift income and assets to jurisdictions that are not participants to information sharing agreements (Johannesen and Zucman, 2014). Ensuring the comprehensiveness and density of the network of information sharing agreements will be an important part of enhancing the success. As AEOI has only begun in 2017, no detailed statistical studies have been conducted on its impact, though countries have already received close to EUR 80 billion in unplanned additional revenue as a result of voluntary disclosure programmes and other similar initiatives in the lead-up to the first exchanges (OECD, 2017b).

Some countries have continued to gradually raise tax rates on dividends and interest. Belgium, Finland, Greece, Luxembourg, Norway, the Slovak Republic and Sweden introduced tax rate increases on dividends and interest taking effect in 2016 and 2017, while Argentina and Ireland lowered tax rates (Table 3.6). Some countries introduced base changes (Table 3.7). In 2016, Sweden broadened the capital income tax base for dividends, interest and bond investment income while Iceland, the Slovak Republic and South Africa implemented base narrowing measures. Estonia and the United Kingdom introduced changes to their dividend and interest tax base which entered into force in 2017: Estonia abolished an interest tax exemption and the United Kingdom removed the withholding obligation for interest paid by collective investment vehicles and on peer to peer loans.

Table 3.6. **Changes to tax rates on capital income introduced in 2016**

	Rate ⇧		Rate ⇩	
Into effect in	2016	2017 or later	2016	2017 or later
Dividend or interest income/equity or bond investment	BEL FIN GRC NOR SWE	BEL LUX NOR SVK	ARG	IRL
Capital gains	AUT KOR		ARG GBR IRL*	IRL*
Rental income	GRC			
Tax treatment of pensions and savings accounts				FIN
Employee share acquisition deductions				

* In Ireland, the reduced rate of tax on capital gains is a specific relief available only on disposals of certain assets by entrepreneurs.

Source: OECD Annual Tax Policy Reform Questionnaire.

Table 3.7. **Changes to capital income tax bases introduced in 2016**

	Base ⇧		Base ⇩	
Into effect in	2016	2017 or later	2016	2017 or later
Dividend or interest income/equity or bond investment	SWE	EST	ISL SVK ZAF	(GBR)
Capital gains	BEL		ARG	BEL
Rental income	EST SWE		ISL	
Tax treatment of pensions and savings accounts	CAN	AUS EST GBR (NLD) ZAF	EST KOR MEX PRT ZAF	AUS CZE EST FIN ISL LUX PRT
Employee share acquisition deductions	GBR		AUT	

Note: Countries in brackets have only announced reforms.

The tax rate increases on dividend income introduced in several countries seem to follow a broader post-crisis trend. The overall tax burden on dividend income is a combination of the taxation of profits at the corporate level and taxes at the personal shareholder level. These may include income taxes, withholding taxes, and taxes on presumptive rates of return (Harding, 2013). Figure 3.8 shows that the total tax burden on dividend income has increased slightly since the crisis, in contrast with the pre-crisis period during which the tax burden on dividend income generally decreased. The post-crisis rise in dividend taxation has been the result of increased taxation at the shareholder level while corporate tax rates have continued to decrease modestly. Nevertheless, there were still wide differences in the ways OECD countries taxed dividends in 2016 (Figure 3.8).

Figure 3.8. **Combined top statutory tax rates on dividend income**

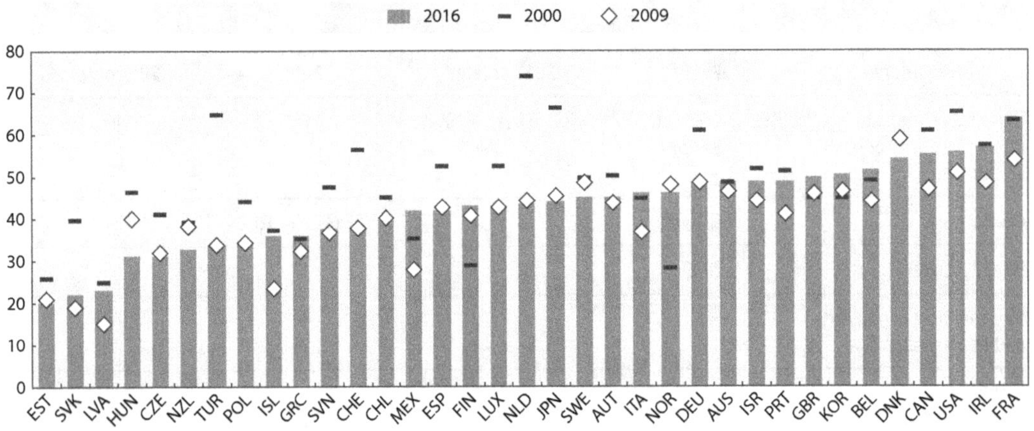

Source: OECD Tax Database, www.oecd.org/tax/tax-policy/tax-database.htm.

The Netherlands introduced important changes to the taxation of personal capital income. Instead of taxing the actual income from savings, the Netherlands includes in its personal capital income tax base a pre-set notional return levied on worldwide assets net of liabilities (except for owner-occupied immovable property). Prior to 1 January 2017, net assets were deemed to earn a notional return of 4%. This notional return was then taxed at a flat 30% rate. As of 1 January 2017, the notional return of 4% was replaced by differential notional returns, depending on the taxpayers' wealth. For 2017, the following notional returns apply: 2.87% on the part of total assets with a value of EUR 25 000 to EUR 100 000, 4.60% on the part of total assets with a value of EUR 100 000 to EUR 1 million, and 5.39% on the part of total assets with a value exceeding EUR 1 million. These fixed returns continue to be taxed at a flat rate of 30%. The basic allowance deducted from the taxable base was also increased to EUR 25 000 (double for married couples and partners).

An increasing number of countries are reforming the way they tax pensions and savings accounts, often in an attempt to increase the fairness of tax privileges. In 2016, eight countries implemented changes to the taxation of pension contributions and savings accounts. These reforms, with the exception of Canada which limited annual contributions to tax-free savings accounts, narrowed tax bases by increasing tax allowances, exemptions or allowing deductions. In addition, nine countries introduced reforms which came into force in 2017. Finland is the only country that reduced its overall tax rate on pension savings by lowering the surtax levied on pensions. All the other countries have reformed the pension tax base. Australia introduced a cap on the amount of capital that can be transferred to the tax-free earnings retirement phase of superannuation, reduced the concessional and non-concessional contributions caps, and removed the tax exemption in respect of transitions to retirement income streams. Estonia increased the pension tax-free allowance for 2017, but abolished it from 2018 onwards. The United Kingdom reduced the money purchase annual allowance (MPAA) – the amount individuals can contribute to the defined contribution pension scheme after having previously received a pension. South Africa disallowed the tax exemption for retirement funds not located within the country. Other countries like the Czech Republic, Estonia, Finland, Iceland and Luxembourg increased pension deductions or allowances and Portugal abolished its extraordinary solidarity contribution on pensions.

3.2 Corporate income tax and other corporate taxes

Corporate tax revenues have not recovered to pre-crisis levels

Corporate tax revenues account for a comparatively modest share of total tax revenues in the group of countries surveyed. In OECD countries, CIT revenues accounted for, on average, around 8.8% of total tax revenues in 2014. This is a much smaller share compared to other revenue sources such as PIT (24%), SSCs (26.2%) and VAT (20.1%). However, countries have different tax mixes and the importance of CIT revenues varies significantly across countries: in 2015, the share of CIT in total tax revenues ranged from just 4.0% in Slovenia to 23.7% in Chile.

Corporate tax revenues have increased slowly since the end of the crisis. Revenues from CIT tend to be more responsive to the business cycle than revenues from other taxes. Average CIT revenues in the OECD increased to around 3.6% of GDP in 2007, just before the onset of the economic crisis. Subsequently, the average dropped to 2.6% in 2009 and then recovered slightly over the following years, reaching 2.9% of GDP in 2015, which is below pre-crisis levels but close to the average CIT-to-GDP ratio in the early 2000s. Going beyond the average, the data shows that CIT revenues as a share of GDP dropped in all but five countries (Estonia, Greece, Luxembourg, Mexico and Turkey) in 2008 and 2009 but that a majority of 24 countries recorded an average increase in CIT revenues of 0.6 percentage points relative to GDP in the 2010-15 period. Norway, Luxembourg and South Africa were the only countries that experienced significant revenue decreases (Figure 3.9).

Figure 3.9. **CIT revenues as a share of GDP by country**

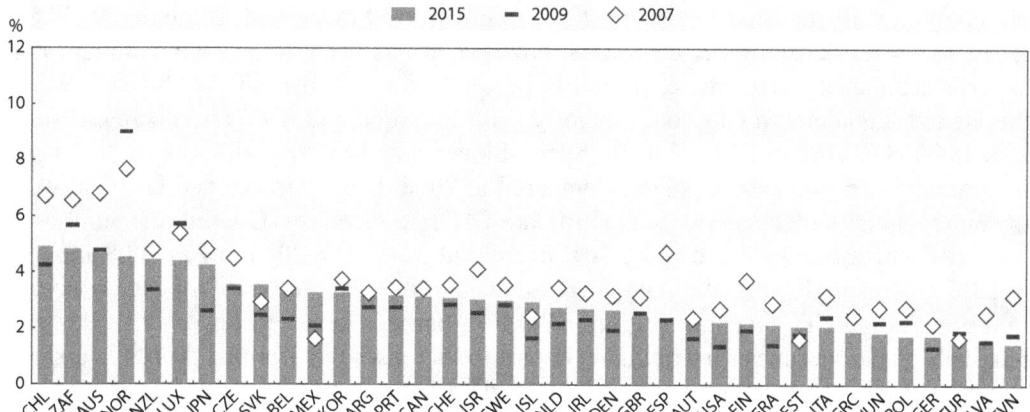

Source: Regional Revenue Statistics databases (www.oecd.org/tax/tax-policy/revenue-statistics-comparable-tax-revenue-data.htm).

Last year's CIT trends have intensified

Last year's report concluded that the trend of decreasing statutory CIT rates which had slowed down after the economic crisis was gaining renewed momentum. In 2015, Estonia implemented a CIT rate reduction while Japan, Spain, Norway and Israel legislated CIT rate reductions which came into force in 2016. In addition, CIT rates targeted to small- and medium-sized enterprises (SMEs) were reduced in several countries and some countries introduced preferential regimes for IP-related income. Reductions in CIT rates were accompanied by mixed corporate tax base developments. On the one hand, countries reported base narrowing provisions, in particular through R&D tax incentives and accelerated depreciation, in an effort to stimulate innovation and increase investment. On the other hand, many countries broadened their corporate tax bases through the adoption of measures aimed at curbing international tax avoidance.

This year's report confirms the direction of CIT reforms and suggests that some of these developments have in fact intensified. Eight countries introduced standard CIT rate cuts, averaging 2.7 percentage points, which became effective in 2017 and three have announced standard CIT rate reductions in the future (Figure 3.12 and Table 3.8). In many countries, these cuts are expected to have significant negative revenue effects. In addition, seven countries have legislated or announced CIT rate reductions for SMEs entering into force in 2017 or later (Table 3.8). Interestingly as well, many of the countries that implemented CIT rate cuts have done so through gradual or multi-year cuts. There are a few countries, however, most notably Hungary, that introduced or announced very significant and sudden CIT rate decreases. Only two countries (Chile and Slovenia) increased their statutory CIT rates. This renewed CIT rate competition can in part be viewed as a response to weak investment in many countries (see Chapter 1). This year's report also points to increasing tax competition through new or enhanced incentives, in particular for R&D and IP-related activities. Base broadening reforms, on the other hand, generally involved continued efforts to address international tax avoidance through progress in the implementation of the BEPS package and limitations to existing loss-carry forward provisions.

Corporate income tax rates continued to fall

CIT rates are lower in many countries than a decade ago. Figure 3.10 shows the continuous fall of the average standard CIT rate in OECD countries from 32.2% in 2000 to 24.7% in 2016. Figure 3.11 looks at the changes in CIT rates by country since 2008. Countries are ranked by their CIT rates in 2016, showing that the United States remained the country with the highest rate in 2016, followed by France and Belgium. At 39.5% Japan had a similarly high rate in 2008; however, it has been among the countries that experienced the largest decrease, around 10 percentage points, over the last 8 years. While the United Kingdom was the only country with a comparable CIT rate decrease, from 28% in 2008 to 20% in 2016, Finland, Spain, Slovenia and Sweden all reduced their rates by around 5 to 6 percentage points. Compared to 2008, Chile, Greece and Portugal were the only countries that experienced significant CIT rate increases. Overall, the number of countries with a statutory rate above 30% decreased from 21 in 2000 to 7 in 2008 and to 5 in 2016. Interestingly, this continual decrease in statutory CIT rates has not been reflected in a decrease in CIT revenues (Figure 3.9). This paradox between lower CIT rates and relatively stable revenues is attributable in part to increases in corporate profits as a share of national income but further work is needed to better understand it (Piotrowska and Vanborren, 2008).

Figure 3.10. **Unweighted average CIT rate and CIT revenues in OECD countries, 2000 to 2016**

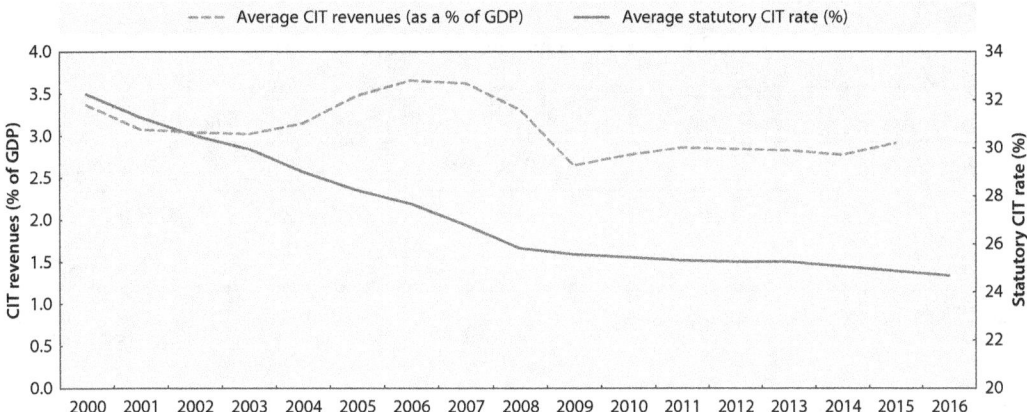

Source: OECD Tax Database (www.oecd.org/tax/tax-policy/tax-database.htm) and OECD Revenue Statistics (http://dx.doi.org/10.1787/data-00262-en).

Figure 3.11. **Standard CIT rates in 2008, 2011 and 2016 and CIT rates on intellectual property**

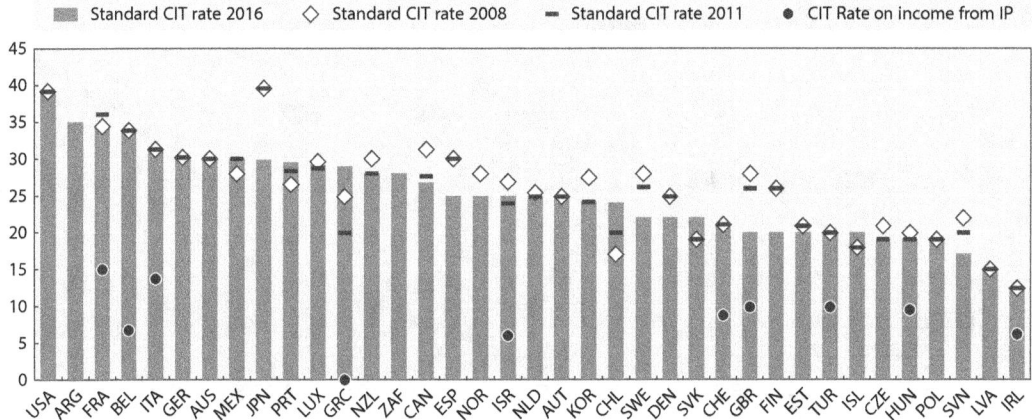

Note: standard CIT rates include sub-central government CIT rates

Source: OECD Tax Database, www.oecd.org/tax/tax-policy/tax-database.htm and IBFD.

Several countries implemented multi-year CIT rate cuts which started or were already effective in 2016. In Spain, the CIT rate was reduced from 30% to 28% in 2015 and to 25% in 2016. In Norway, a CIT rate reduction by 2 percentage points became effective in 2016. In order to further reduce the gap with statutory tax rates in other countries, an additional reduction in the CIT rate from 25% to 24% entering into force in January 2017 was adopted. As highlighted in the previous report, Japan committed to a comprehensive corporate tax reform package aimed at making its corporate tax system more growth-friendly. While successive CIT rate reductions were brought into effect in 2015 and 2016, further reductions will enter into force in 2018. Taken together, these changes amount to a reduction of the statutory CIT rate from 25.5% in 2014 to 23.4% in 2016 and 23.2% in 2018; in line with these changes the standard local enterprise taxes rates were also lowered from 7.2% in 2014 to 3.6% in 2016. Finally, Israel continued its gradual CIT rate reduction. After a CIT rate reduction from 26.5% to 25% in 2016 and given positive tax revenue developments, the CIT rate was further lowered to 24% in 2017 and will be cut to 23% in 2018.

Table 3.8. **CIT rate changes introduced in 2016**

Into effect in	Rate ⇧		Rate ⇩	
	2016	2017 or later	2016	2017 or later
Standard CIT rate	CHL	SVN	ESP ISR JPN NOR	(AUS) (EST) (FRA) GBR HUN ISR ITA JPN LUX NOR SVK
SME CIT rate			(AUS)* CAN	(AUS) FRA HUN LUX NLD POL PRT

Notes: Countries in brackets have only announced reforms.
* In Australia, the rate reduction for small businesses has not been enacted. If the reform is legislated, it will apply retroactively to activity dating back to 1 July 2016.

Source: OECD Annual Tax Policy Reform Questionnaire.

Figure 3.12. **Changes to central statutory CIT rates implemented or legislated in 2016**

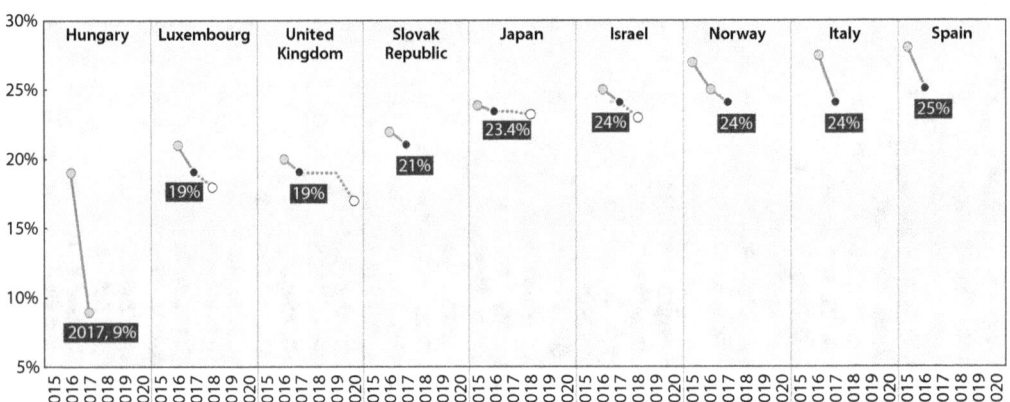

Source: OECD Annual Tax Policy Reform Questionnaire.

Gradual cuts in CIT rates will continue in 2017 and beyond (Figure 3.12). As part of a broader reform, Luxembourg introduced a gradual CIT rate reduction from 21% to 19% in 2017 and will go to 18% in 2018 (Box 3.4). In addition, the reduced rate structure for firms below certain turnover thresholds was adjusted to reduce the tax burden on smaller businesses.[4] The Slovak Republic reduced its CIT rate from 22% to 21% as of January 2017. Additional rate cuts may be considered at a later date. In the United Kingdom, the 2015 Summer Budget included a CIT rate reduction from 20% to 19% from April 2017 and then to 18% from April 2020. In the 2016 Budget, it was announced that the CIT rate would be reduced to 17% rather than 18% from April 2020. In France, the Finance Bill adopted in December 2016 includes a progressive reduction of the standard CIT rate from 33.3% to 28%. From January 2017, the new 28% rate will only apply to SMEs on the first EUR 75 000 of taxable income. Australia, in its 2016–17 Budget, announced a progressive CIT rate reduction from 30% to 25%, starting with a reduction in the small business tax rate from 28.5% to 27.5% for the 2016–17 income year. The turnover threshold to qualify for the lower rate would start at AUD 10 million and progressively rise until the 27.5% rate applies to all corporate entities subject to the standard CIT rate in 2023–24. The CIT rate would then be cut to 27% for 2024–25 and by one percentage point in each subsequent year until it reaches 25% for the 2026–27 income year. These gradual CIT rate cuts can be viewed in part as a way to allow smoother budget adjustments.

> ### Box 3.4. Luxembourg's comprehensive tax reform
>
> In December 2016, Luxembourg enacted a comprehensive tax reform. The reform was designed to increase fairness, support investment, enhance competitiveness, strengthen entrepreneurship and innovation, encourage consumption and savings, and boost economic growth. It consists of several components which generally became effective in 2017.
>
> First, significant corporate tax changes were introduced. The CIT rate was reduced from 21% to 19% in 2017 and will be further lowered to 18% in 2018. A limit to the carry-forward of losses was introduced: losses incurred during and after 2017 can only be carried forward for a maximum of 17 years, whereas no limitation in time applied previously. To support investment, the investment tax credits were raised. The tax credit for the recruitment of unemployed persons was extended until December 2019. Also, upon request, taxpayers are now allowed to defer the depreciation allowance and, if not used before, must be fully used at the end of the useful life of the asset. The minimum net worth tax was increased (from EUR 3 210 to EUR 4 815), and a mandatory electronic filing system is now in place for CIT returns, municipal business tax returns and net worth tax returns.
>
> In the area of personal taxes, PIT brackets and rates were modified, with the introduction of new brackets and two additional top marginal rates. The 0.5% temporary tax for the budget balance was abolished. The tax credits for employees, self-employed and pensioners as well as the tax credits and allowances for expenses for children not residing with their parents and the tax credits for single-parents were raised. A number of measures were introduced to support homeownership including an increase in the ceiling for deductible contributions to home savings schemes and an increase in the ceiling for mortgage interest deductions. Starting in 2018, married couples will have the option to file separate tax returns, and the taxation for non-residents was aligned with the tax regime applicable to residents. Finally, withholding taxes on qualifying interests were increased from 10% to 20%.
>
> The VAT regime was also amended. *De jure* or *de facto* directors and managers in charge of the daily management of a company are now responsible for the fulfilment of the company's VAT obligations and personally and jointly liable for a negligent breach of their obligations (e.g. late payment, inaccurate VAT returns). Penalties for VAT fraud were also increased and progressive criminal responsibility was introduced in case of aggravated tax fraud.
>
> Luxembourg also introduced environmentally related tax measures. A EUR 5 000 tax allowance was introduced for the purchase of an electric or hydrogen-powered car, and the benefit in kind in case of car leases granted by an employer was increased by a progressive rate depending on the car's CO_2 emissions.

Other countries adopted a less gradual approach, introducing or announcing significant rate reductions in comparatively short time periods. The most significant change was introduced in Hungary, where a CIT rate reduction from 19% to 9% came into force in January 2017. This policy is aimed at increasing the attractiveness of Hungary as a destination for foreign investment and is combined with a set of related tax measures (Box 3.5). Among other measures, the reform package included rate changes for SMEs. In Hungary, small businesses can, under certain circumstances, opt out of the CIT and employer social insurance contributions, choosing instead to pay a small business tax which is levied on the sum of dividend pay-outs, gross salaries and the balance of the capital changes. In parallel to the decrease in the standard CIT rate and the Social Contribution Tax rate, the small business tax rate was reduced from 16% to 14% in 2017. In Italy, as included in the 2016 Budget Law, the central government CIT rate was reduced from 27.5% to 24% as of 1 January 2017. Finally, a significant decrease in the CIT rate has been announced in Estonia, where corporate income is only taxed upon distribution while income retained in the company is not taxable. After lowering the rate by one percentage point in 2015, the government announced another decrease in the tax rate from 20% to 14%. Although this reform would represent a substantial rate reduction, revenue effects are expected to be more than compensated by a simultaneous, but not yet detailed, change in the corporate tax base.

Box 3.5. **Hungary's package of tax reforms**

In 2016, the Hungarian Parliament adopted several tax reforms aimed at simplifying the tax system, increasing equity and fairness, boosting economic growth and supporting investment. Most of the measures entered into force on 1 January 2017. The main provisions included mainly:

- A reduction of the CIT to a flat rate of 9%, which is a significant change from the previous progressive tax system whereby the first HUF 500 million of taxable income were taxed at 10% and the excess at 19%;

- A reduction in the PIT rate for self-entrepreneurs;

- A reduction of the small business tax (KIVA tax) rate from 16% to 14% for 2017, and to 13% from 2018 onwards;

- An increase in the upper yearly revenue limit from HUF 6 million to HUF 12 million from 2017 for the lump sum tax on small enterprises (KATA);

- The introduction of a tax allowance of three times the investment made in registered start-up enterprises;

- The introduction of new tax credits for investments increasing energy efficiency;

- The elimination of the surtax on financial credit institutions;

- A reduction of the employer SSC rate from 27% to 22% in 2017, which will be further reduced to 20% in 2018. Further cuts – amounting to 8.5 percentage points in total – have been planned for subsequent years (2018-22) depending on wage developments;

- A reduction in the number of health care contribution rates from 5 to 2, and a reduction in the top rate from 27% to 22% in 2017, which will be further reduced to 20% in 2018;

The reduction of the VAT rate for different goods and services (e.g. poultry, eggs, fresh milk, catering in restaurants) and an increase in the VAT exemption threshold.

Only two countries raised their statutory CIT rates. Chile continued to gradually increase its CIT rate as part of a comprehensive tax reform that was legislated in 2014. Slovenia adjusted its CIT rate upwards, from 17% to 19% in January 2017, in order to neutralise the revenue loss resulting from changes in PIT and achieve financial consolidation. Other rate increases were targeted at specific tax bases such as petroleum income in Norway and gaming income in Greece; similarly, Belgium introduced a new tax on income earned in the diamond sector which entered into force in 2016.

While CIT rate reductions are all associated with significant negative revenue effects, rate increases are expected to contribute only marginally to public budgets. The most relevant revenue raising reforms were thus, apart from some base broadening reforms which are discussed below, the two CIT rate increases as well as some of the newly introduced taxes. This includes, in particular, a new tax levied on financial activities in Norway which is intended to counterbalance the VAT exemption for the financial service sector. The reform entails a 5% tax on employee compensation engaged in financial activities and excludes firms in the financial sector from the general CIT rate reductions, implying that the rate will remain at 25% (the 5% payroll tax would be deductible from the CIT base).

Many countries enhanced their business tax incentives, in particular for R&D and innovation

In 2016, many countries introduced enhanced or new tax incentives for businesses, driven by growth stimulus and tax competition objectives. Promoting investment was a key policy goal. Many countries reported the adoption of base narrowing reforms which were mostly aimed at increasing business investment, either through general tax incentives available for all types of investments and businesses, or through tax incentives targeted specifically at investments in R&D or environmentally related projects (Table 3.9).

Table 3.9. **CIT base changes introduced in 2016**

	Base ⇧		Base ⇩	
Into effect in	2016	2017 or later	2016	2017 or later
Depreciation allowances	JPN	NOR		ITA
Loss-carry forward provisions	ESP JPN	ESP JPN KOR LAT LUX (GBR)		
Anti-avoidance rules	AUS IRL NLD ZAF	(EST) (GBR) NLD POL SWE		
General investment incentives			TUR	FRA LUX
R&D tax incentives			AUT TUR	HUN ISL ITA MEX POL
Environmentally related tax incentives				HUN MEX (GBR)
SME-related tax incentives				POL PRT

Note: Countries in brackets have only announced reforms.

Source: OECD Annual Tax Policy Reform Questionnaire.

Some countries expanded general investment tax incentives. Luxembourg increased its investment tax credits. The country offers two types of general investment tax credits, a global tax credit for tangible depreciable assets and a supplementary tax credit which is calculated on an incremental basis; both credits are non-refundable but can be carried forward and offset against taxable income earned in the following 10 years. To further attract international investment, both credits were increased by one percentage point, to 8% and 13% respectively. Since these tax credits are not targeted to specific investments or businesses, this reform results in an overall reduction in effective tax rates on investments in Luxembourg.

As part of its new industrial plan, Italy extended its super-depreciation scheme and introduced a new hyper-depreciation scheme for certain high-technology assets. The 2017 Budget Law extended the extra 40% depreciation deduction (i.e. total tax depreciation of up to 140% of the cost) for tangible assets whose depreciation rate for tax purposes exceeds 6.5%. In addition, the Budget Law introduces an extra 150% depreciation (i.e. total tax depreciation of up to 250% of the cost) for certain high-technology assets.

Turkey announced the introduction of a "super tax incentive model" which would allow the government to grant comprehensive tax incentives to specific investments on a project basis. Although the types of investments that will be supported have not been determined yet, possible benefits include corporate tax exemptions for up to 10 years as well as different forms of direct government support. In addition to this general incentive, Turkey introduced a specific 50% tax allowance for qualifying R&D expenditures and made expenses related to design activities and personnel eligible for the same tax incentive.

A number of countries introduced new or enhanced provisions for R&D or IP-related activities. Government support for business R&D is intended to encourage firms to invest in knowledge that can result in innovations that transform markets and benefit society through positive spillover effects. Public support is justified because of the market failures typically associated with business R&D, in particular the difficulties firms face in not being able to fully appropriate the returns to their investment and the difficulties associated with obtaining finance for risky projects, especially for small start-ups. Tax incentives for business R&D can be granted either in the form of a preferential tax treatment of R&D expenditure (expenditure-based provisions) or a preferential treatment of incomes from licensing or asset disposal attributable to R&D or patents (income-based provisions). Income-based provisions have been less common than expenditure-based provisions but have received increased interest in recent years (Figure 3.11). They have also been a source of concern, in particular in the case of IP boxes, as they tend to benefit larger companies and can, if not designed properly, be used by companies to artificially shift profits across jurisdictions (Appelt et al., 2016).

Several reforms aimed at enhancing the generosity of existing expenditure-based R&D tax provisions. Austria increased its volume-based R&D tax credit from 10% to 12% as of January 2016. Iceland legislated a more generous change to its incentive scheme, tripling the ceiling for its refundable 20% R&D tax credit as of June 2016. Mexico introduced a new incremental R&D tax credit of 30%, which entered into force in January 2017. Norway increased the upper limits of eligible in-house and procured R&D expenditures under its existing tax incentive system. Poland increased the generosity of its R&D support scheme through a range of measures, including the deductibility of expenses incurred for obtaining patents, increases in the shares of deductible qualifying expenses for SMEs and larger enterprises, a prolongation of the time period during which R&D expenditures can be deducted as well as the refundability of the tax credit for start-up companies. In Italy, the R&D tax credit was extended until 2020 and increased to 50% (previously 25% or 50% depending on the type of cost) of the annual R&D expenditure exceeding the average spending of fiscal years 2012, 2013 and 2014. The annual cap was also increased from EUR 5 million to EUR 20 million.

Belgium, Ireland and Israel introduced new preferential income tax rates for IP-related activities. Taking into account the nexus approach under BEPS Action 5, which allows taxpayers to benefit from an IP regime only to the extent that they have themselves incurred qualifying R&D expenditures that gave rise to the IP income, Ireland introduced a new preferential regime which became effective in January 2016. The Irish Knowledge

Development Box offers an effective CIT rate of 6.25% on profits arising from certain IP assets which are the result of qualifying R&D activities carried out in Ireland. In Belgium, the "patent income deduction" regime was repealed in July 2016, with a grandfather rule for five years, and replaced with a new "innovation income deduction". In Israel, the new IP regime offers a reduced CIT rate of 6% on IP-based income and on capital gains from future sales of IP. The 6% rate applies to qualifying Israeli companies that are part of a group with global consolidated revenue of over ILS 10 billion (USD 2.5 billion). Other qualifying companies with global consolidated revenue below ILS 10 billion are subject to a 12% tax rate. Additionally, dividends paid by qualifying companies are subject to a reduced 4% withholding tax. Israel also expanded its existing tax incentives for "preferred enterprises" and "special preferred enterprises" which offer reduced CIT rates to large enterprises that meet certain investment requirements. Together with the reduction in the standard CIT rate discussed above, these tax incentives aim at strengthening Israel's attractiveness for IP investments.

Finally, Hungary introduced a tax allowance for companies investing in registered start-ups. The new legislation became effective in January 2017 and allows investing companies to deduct up to three times the amount of the investment over the following three years; to limit revenue losses, the allowance is subject to a ceiling.

Enhanced tax incentives were also used to promote employment and green investments

France raised the rate of its tax credit aimed at boosting competitiveness and employment (CICE) from 6% to 7%. The measure became effective in 2017. The CICE is available to all companies and seeks to enhance the competitiveness of the French economy. This tax credit is equal to a percentage of each company's payroll (excluding wages exceeding two-and-a-half times the French minimum wage) and can be directly deducted from CIT liability. The new rate of 7% will apply to wages paid as from January 2017.

Three countries also reported tax incentives aimed at promoting green investments. Hungary implemented a new tax credit in 2017 for investments increasing energy efficiency, amounting to up to 30% of eligible investment costs. In Mexico, a 30% tax credit for investments in recharging equipment for electric vehicles entered into force in January 2017, while the United Kingdom announced a one-year tax break for companies investing in charge-points for electric vehicles. All these incentives are intended to encourage a shift towards renewable energies, thereby reducing negative externalities associated with the use of carbon-intensive energy sources.

Some countries introduced tax measures targeted at SMEs

Some countries implemented reforms to reduce the tax burden on SMEs. As discussed in the previous report, Canada reduced its federal-level small business income tax rate from 11% to 10.5% in January 2016 but further reductions were deferred. In Australia, SMEs will be the first to benefit from CIT rate cuts. Following the initial rate reduction for SMEs, the threshold to qualify for the lower CIT rate will progressively rise until fiscal year 2023-24, when it is scheduled to apply to all corporate entities. Poland introduced a new tax bracket for firms earning less than a certain annual turnover threshold, which entered into force in January 2017 and allows SMEs to benefit from a reduced rate of 15% compared to the statutory rate of 19%. Similarly, the Netherlands committed to a gradual increase of the turnover threshold for the first tax bracket over the next five years, thereby reducing the tax burden on SMEs. Finally, the Slovak Republic enacted the elimination of its minimum tax which will become effective as of January 2018.

Broader sets of measures targeting SMEs were introduced in Argentina, Portugal and New Zealand. New Zealand introduced a combination of administrative tax measures to reduce compliance costs for SMEs. In Portugal, several new measures target SMEs: the special minimum tax was reduced and the CIT rate for SMEs in the first tax bracket was reduced from 17% to 12.5%, provided they are located in geographically disadvantaged areas. The reform package coming into effect in January 2017 also includes an increase in the notional deduction for equity capital increases for SMEs from 5% to 7%. Argentina introduced a comprehensive reform package to support SMEs, consisting of several policy measures entering into force in 2016 and 2017. Among other concessions, it was decided to exempt SMEs from the minimum deemed income tax as of January 2017 and to abolish the tax completely by 2019.

Several countries broadened corporate tax bases in particular by restricting loss-carryover provisions

In contrast with incentive measures which narrow tax bases, countries introduced a number of base broadening reforms, focusing in particular at the domestic level on restricting loss carryover provisions. Spain limited tax loss deductions for large companies for tax periods starting in or after 2016: companies with a net revenue of EUR 60 million or more may only offset 25% of their tax base, while a 50% threshold applies for companies with net revenues between EUR 20 and EUR 60 million. In Japan, limits to the deductibility of corporate tax losses were successively reduced from 65% of taxable income to 60% in 2016 and 55% in 2017. Korea introduced a limit to tax loss deductions of 80% of taxable income for foreign companies, thereby aligning rules for foreign and domestic companies. As of January 2017, Latvia introduced a 75% deduction limit, while Luxembourg has limited the period for which tax losses can be carried forward from indefinitely to 17 years. The United Kingdom introduced in its latest Budget two separate measures, one which facilitates the use of tax losses in group consolidation, and the other which restricts yearly deductions to 50% of taxable income (for banks, their ability to offset losses will be reduced from 50% to 25% of annual taxable profits). However, in terms of revenue impacts, the effect of the second measure is expected to prevail.

In these countries, restrictions to loss carryover rules are expected to raise significant revenues. No interest mark-ups are typically provided on tax losses as they are carried forward over time; corporate tax systems are therefore non-neutral across investments with different risk profiles. Introducing further restrictions, through time or deduction limits, exacerbates this feature. Although such restrictions may be less relevant for entities within a corporate group, due to the possibility of group-level consolidation, it may have significant impacts on domestic firms which are often smaller, possibly credit-constrained and generally less able to absorb fluctuations in business performance or macroeconomic conditions (Hanappi, forthcoming).

Additional domestic base broadening measures were reported. Japan simplified its tax depreciation system as part of its comprehensive corporate tax reform in 2016 but Norway was so far the only country to broaden its corporate tax base by reducing accelerated depreciation in 2017. In particular, the supplementary first-year allowance for investments in machinery was abolished as of January 2017, which is expected to generate a significant increase in public revenues which could partly offset revenue losses from CIT rate reductions. Apart from possible revenue considerations, the reform was intended to bring tax depreciation in line with economic depreciation, thereby increasing the neutrality of the corporate tax system. In Italy, the rate to calculate the notional return to equity of the allowance for corporate equity (ACE) regime was first reduced from 4.75% to 2.3% in 2017 and then increased again to 2.7% in 2018, which has the effect of broadening the CIT base.

Efforts to curb international tax avoidance continued

As was the case last year, many base broadening reforms were aimed at limiting international tax avoidance. Comparing the expected revenue changes within and across countries reveals that some of the largest positive impacts of all identified tax reforms are expected to come from these measures. Many of the reforms announced and legislated in 2016 were driven by the outcomes of the BEPS project (Box 3.6).[5] Countries participating in the Inclusive Framework on BEPS, which brings together almost 100 jurisdictions on

---

Box 3.6. Recommended policy measures to address BEPS

In October 2015, the final package of BEPS measures was endorsed by G20 leaders in Antalya. The final BEPS package includes recommendations on minimum standards, best practices, common approaches and new guidance in key policy areas.

- Minimum standards have been agreed upon in the areas of fighting harmful tax practices (Action 5), preventing treaty abuse (Action 6), Country-by-Country Reporting (Action 13) and improving dispute resolution (Action 14). All participating countries are expected to implement these minimum standards and implementation will be subject to peer review.

- A common approach, which will facilitate the convergence of national practices by interested countries, has been outlined to limit base erosion through interest expenses (Action 4) and to neutralise hybrid mismatches (Action 2). Best practices for countries that seek to strengthen their domestic legislation are provided with the building blocks for effective CFC rules (Action 3) and mandatory disclosure by taxpayers of aggressive or abusive transactions, arrangements or structures (Action 12).

- The permanent establishment (PE) definition in the OECD Model Tax Convention has been changed to restrict inappropriate avoidance of tax nexus through commissionaire arrangements or exploitation of specific exceptions (Action 7). In terms of transfer pricing, important clarifications have been made with regard to delineating the actual transaction, and the treatment of risk and intangibles. More guidance has been provided on several other issues to ensure that transfer pricing outcomes are aligned with value creation (Actions 8-10).

- The changes to the PE definition, the clarifications on transfer pricing, and the guidance on CFC rules are expected to substantially address the BEPS risks exacerbated by the digital economy. Several other options were considered, but not recommended at this stage given the other recommendations and the fact that Value Added Taxes (VAT) will now be levied effectively in the market country facilitating VAT collection (Action 1).

- A multilateral instrument has been developed to facilitate the modification of bilateral tax treaties (Action 15). The modifications made to existing treaties will address the minimum standards against treaty abuse as well as the updated PE definition.

At the February 2016 G20 Finance Ministers meeting, the inclusive framework for the global implementation of the BEPS project was endorsed, with a reiteration of the commitment to timely implementation of the BEPS project and to continue monitoring and addressing BEPS-related issues for a consistent global approach.

an equal footing, have committed to the implementation of the measures recommended under the OECD/G20 BEPS Package, including the four minimum standards: fighting harmful tax practices (Action 5), prevention of treaty abuse (Action 6), Country-by-Country (CbC) reporting (Action 13) and improving dispute resolution (Action 14). All four minimum standards are subject to peer review in order to ensure their timely and accurate implementation.

In anticipation of the peer review process, several countries adjusted their preferential tax regimes. Belgium, Ireland and Israel designed their new preferential IP tax regimes, as discussed above, with the intention of aligning them with the modified nexus approach as defined in the minimum standard under BEPS Action 5. Other countries including Hungary, the Netherlands, Portugal, Switzerland (Canton of Nidwalden) and the United Kingdom, implemented adjustments to their preferential IP regimes in 2016. Based on changes in 2016, the peer review process has cleared IP regimes in Belgium, Hungary, Ireland, the Netherlands, Portugal, the Canton of Nidwalden (Switzerland) and the United Kingdom. The peer review process is still underway and is expected to conclude this year. In addition, in support of these developments, the European Union's code of conduct group on business taxation has adopted the modified nexus approach and is monitoring EU Member States.

Significant progress has also been achieved on CbC reporting. CbC reporting provides a template for multinational enterprises (MNEs) to report high-level transfer pricing related information annually and for each tax jurisdiction in which they do business. The peer review process will be conducted under the supervision of the Inclusive Framework, taking into account the domestic legal and administrative framework as well as agreements on the exchange of information, confidentiality and appropriate use of CbC Reports. Over the course of 2016, around 50 countries adopted CbC reporting or issued related draft legislation (Ernst & Young, 2017).

BEPS Action 14 recommended a set of policy measures to improve countries' capacities to resolve treaty related disputes under the mutual agreement procedure (MAP). The key documents outlining the peer review and monitoring process on dispute resolution were published in October 2016. Peer reviews will be carried out based on a two-stage approach allowing taxpayers to provide inputs on specific areas covering access to MAP, clarity and availability of MAP guidance and the timely implementation of MAP agreements. While newly concluded tax treaties, such as the one between Belgium and Japan, already seek to incorporate BEPS recommendations on dispute resolution, the Multilateral Instrument (MLI) is the main policy measure intended to transpose BEPS recommendations for Actions 6 and 14 into more than 2000 existing tax treaties worldwide.

The MLI will implement minimum standards to counter treaty abuse and improve dispute resolution mechanisms while providing flexibility to accommodate specific tax treaty policies. It will allow countries to update bilateral tax treaties in a flexible and efficient way, thus representing a fundamental change in the way treaties are adapted to changing policy objectives. On 7 June 2017, Ministers and high-level officials from 76 countries and jurisdictions signed or formally expressed their intention to sign the MLI.

The Netherlands and Sweden introduced limits to interest deductibility. These measures became effective in January 2017. In its 2016 Budget, the United Kingdom also announced that it would restrict the tax deductibility of corporate interest expense with effect from 1 April 2017.

Hybrid mismatches can involve either double deductions for the same expense or deductions for an expense without any corresponding receipt being taxable. In the United Kingdom, hybrid mismatch rules were targeted at mismatches from hybrid financial instruments and hybrid entities. The scope of these rules was recently extended through new measures addressing tax avoidance arrangements involving permanent establishments that generate a tax mismatch. South Africa also introduced new hybrid mismatch rules, aimed at eliminating mismatches arising from hybrid debt instruments.

Japan announced in December 2016 substantial changes to its Controlled Foreign Company (CFC) rules. This reform will imply that the approach to recognise tax avoidance risk will no longer rely on a pro-forma basis, i.e. effective tax rates of foreign subsidiaries, but will instead be assessed on the basis of the specific activities and types of income of the relevant subsidiaries; passive income will be subject to tax under the CFC rules, while income generated through real economic activities will be exempt from taxation regardless of foreign subsidiaries' effective tax rates.

In parallel, an Anti-Tax Avoidance Directive was adopted at the European Union (EU) level and a new corporate tax reform package has been proposed by the European Commission (EC). The first Anti-Tax Avoidance Directive (ATAD), ATAD 1, was adopted by the European Council in July 2016 and requires EU Member States to implement some of the BEPS recommendations and introduces a few additional measures. More specifically, it sets out requirements on interest deductibility limitations, exit taxation, a general anti-abuse rule, CFC rules and rules to address intra-EU hybrid mismatches that will enter into force on 1 January 2019. In October 2016, the EC submitted a second ATAD proposal, ATAD 2, to extend the rules against hybrid mismatches to cases involving non-Member States. Along with this proposal, the EC also proposed a two-stage proposal for a common consolidated corporate tax base, which would be a single set of rules to calculate companies' taxable profits in the EU, as well as a Directive on double taxation dispute resolution mechanisms which will reinforce mandatory binding dispute resolution in the EU.

Finally, some countries introduced more unilateral measures to address international tax avoidance. Australia announced the introduction of a Diverted Profits Tax (DPT) to come into force in July 2017, following the United Kingdom which implemented a DPT in 2015. The Australian DPT is a new and separate tax addressing tax avoidance by large companies which are either resident in Australia or have a taxable presence there. Profits earned on the basis of transactions between related entities that fail to meet economic substance requirements will be subject to a 40% tax. The DPT, therefore, acts as a deterrent aimed at increasing CIT revenues as well as preventing tax avoidance.

3.3 VAT/GST and excise duties

VAT revenues have reached record levels

VAT revenues were at an all-time high in OECD countries at 6.8% of GDP and 20.1% of total tax revenues on average in 2014 (excluding the United States which does not have a VAT system) (Figure 3.13). Compared to 2010, revenues from VAT rose as a percentage of GDP in 26 of the 34 OECD countries that operate a VAT as well as in Argentina and South Africa and fell in 8 countries (Figure 3.14). Revenues from excise duties, on the other hand, have been subject to a long-term decline. In 1965, they accounted for 14.2% of total revenues on average in the OECD, compared to 7.6% in 2014 (Figure 3.13).

The increase in VAT revenues partly reflected increases in standard VAT rates. Between 2008 and 2015, the average standard VAT rate in the OECD increased by 1.5 percentage points, from 17.6% to a record level of 19.2% (Figure 3.15). While there were significant differences across countries, standard VAT rates were raised at least once in 21 OECD countries since 2008, and 10 countries now have a standard rate above 22%, against only

Figure 3.13. **VAT and excise tax revenues as a share of total taxation, OECD average, 1965-2014**

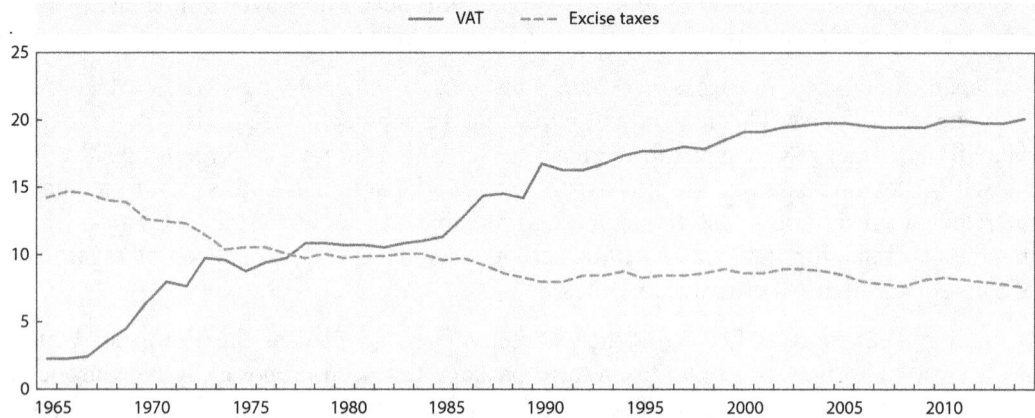

Source: OECD Revenue Statistics, http://dx.doi.org/10.1787/data-00262-en.

Figure 3.14. **VAT revenues as a share of GDP by country in 2000, 2010 and 2015**

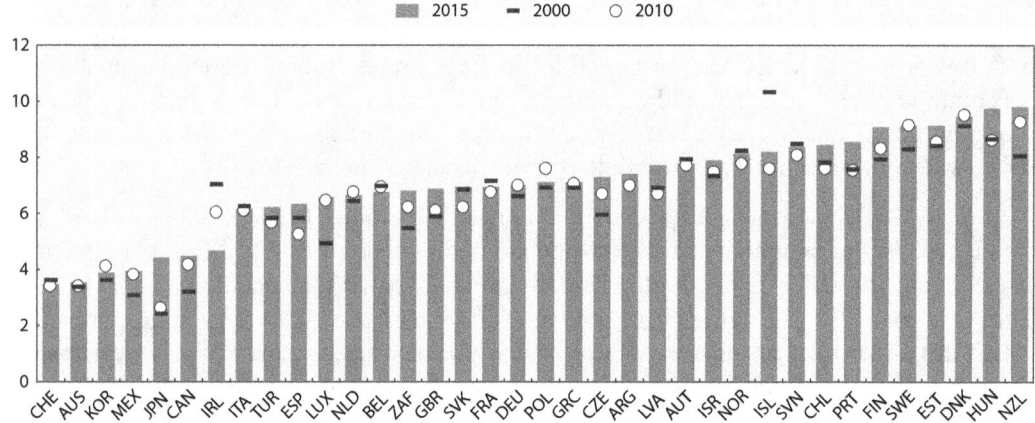

Source: Regional Revenue Statistics databases (www.oecd.org/tax/tax-policy/revenue-statistics-comparable-tax-revenue-data.htm).

Figure 3.15. **Evolution of the OECD average standard VAT rate until January 2017**

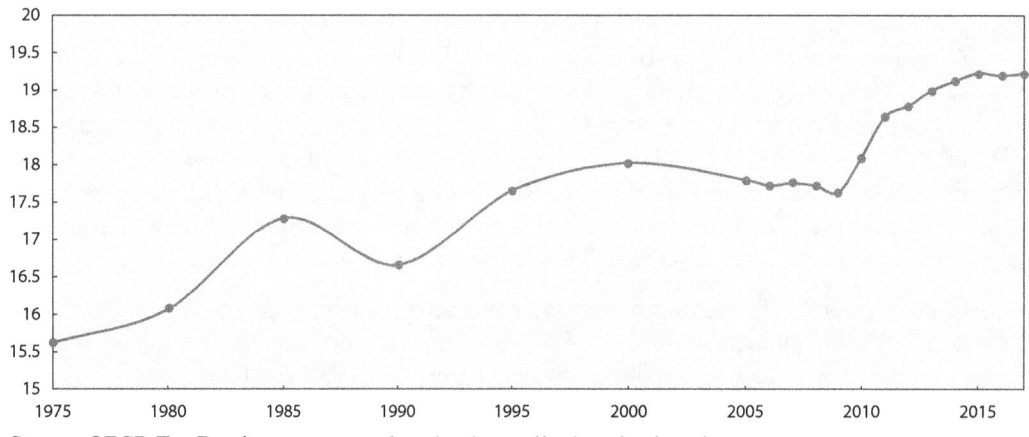

Source: OECD Tax Database, www.oecd.org/tax/tax-policy/tax-database.htm.

four in 2008 (Figure 3.16). Raising standard VAT rates was part of the approach adopted by many countries in the years following the crisis to achieve fiscal consolidation as VAT rate increases provide immediate revenue impacts but do not directly impact competitiveness and are considered less detrimental to economic growth than direct taxes (OECD, 2010). However, the trend towards increasing standard VAT rates did not continue after 2015, with a stabilisation of the average standard VAT rate (OECD, 2016a).

Figure 3.16. **Standard VAT rates by country in 2008 and 2017**

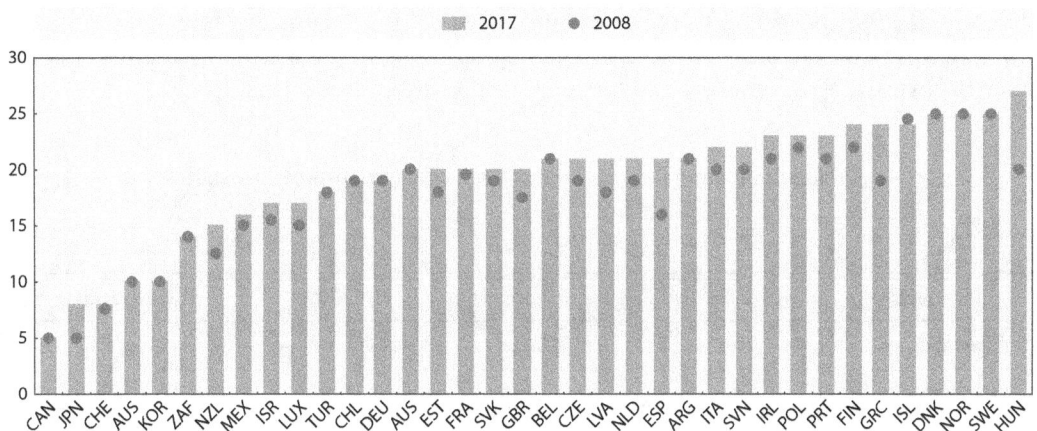

Source: OECD Tax Database, www.oecd.org/tax/tax-policy/tax-database.htm.

Increases in VAT revenues also partly reflected the adoption of measures aimed at broadening VAT bases and at strengthening VAT compliance. As discussed in last year's report, a number of OECD countries broadened their VAT bases by raising their reduced VAT rates and/or by reducing their scope. These reforms were often in line with the findings and recommendations of the OECD on the distributional effects of consumption taxes as they focused on scaling back reduced rates that are inefficient and, in some cases, regressive in the sense that they provide greater benefits to richer households in both aggregate and relative terms (OECD/KIPF, 2014). Several countries also introduced measures to counter VAT fraud and to strengthen VAT compliance with a view to increasing VAT collection (OECD, 2016a).

In general, compared to previous years, the focus of VAT reforms has shifted away from rate increases. Apart from Greece which raised its standard VAT rate, there were no changes to standard VAT rates in 2016 in the countries surveyed. There were some reforms related to reduced VAT rates but those often had the effect of narrowing VAT bases. A trend in many countries was the increase of VAT registration or collection thresholds. Significant reforms were also adopted or announced regarding the application of VAT in the digital sector.

With regard to excise duties, there were many tax increases, in particular on tobacco products. Reported reforms and reform plans also confirmed the increasing popularity of taxes on soft drinks. This year's report suggests that excise duties are increasingly being used to influence consumer behaviour, in particular to improve health by taxing more heavily unhealthy consumption.

Countries are no longer resorting to increases in standard VAT rates

Very little happened to standard VAT rates in 2016, suggesting that countries are no longer increasing standard VAT rates to raise additional revenue, which may reflect the fact that VAT rates have already reached high levels in many countries. Greece was the only country that reported an increase in its standard VAT rate, which was raised from 23% to 24% on 1 June 2016 (Table 3.10). Japan decided to postpone its consumption tax rate increase from 8% to 10%, which was initially set to come into force in 2017, until October 2019. In Italy, the plan to raise the standard VAT rate from 22% to 24% was abandoned. In its 2017 Budget law, Italy nevertheless confirmed potential standard VAT rate increases (from 22% to 24% on 1 January 2018 and then to 25.9% in 2019) if the country does not meet its budget targets. In Canada, there were several increases in the provincial components of the Harmonised Sales Tax (in New Brunswick, Newfoundland and Labrador, and Prince Edward Island).

Table 3.10. **Changes to standard VAT rates introduced in 2016**

	Rate ⇧		Rate ⇩	
Into effect in	2016	2017 or later	2016	2017 or later
Standard VAT rate	GRC	(ITA) JPN		

Note: Countries in brackets have only announced reforms.
Source: OECD Annual Tax Policy Reform Questionnaire.

None of the countries surveyed lowered their standard VAT rate. Poland abandoned its plan to reduce the standard VAT rate from 23% to 22%. The VAT rate was raised in January 2011 as a temporary measure to help contain the budget deficit but the return to the 22% rate has since been postponed several times. Overall, the OECD average standard VAT rate increased very slightly, reflecting only the VAT rate increase in Greece (Figure 3.15).

The use of reduced VAT rates was expanded in a number of countries

Some countries broadened their VAT bases by increasing reduced VAT rates or by reducing their scope. In Norway, the increase in the reduced VAT rate from 8% to 10%, which applies to passenger transport, accommodation, public service broadcasting and cinema, became effective in 2016. Similarly, in Austria, the increase in the reduced VAT rate from 10% to 13% for cultural events, hotel accommodation, domestic air travel, and specific supplies such as plants and certain animal feeds, came into force in 2016. Greece extended the standard VAT rate to the last group of islands which benefited from the 30% VAT rate discount. Belgium removed the VAT exemption for online gambling and cash games other than lotteries. Finally, there were plans to increase the accommodation VAT rate from 9% to 14% in Estonia but those plans were abandoned.

A number of countries, on the other hand, broadened the scope of their reduced VAT rates, in particular to support social goals. The Slovak Republic and Turkey lowered VAT rates on selected foodstuffs in 2016. In Hungary and Portugal, some basic food items became subject to lower VAT rates on 1 January 2017. In Hungary, the introduction of a reduced VAT rate on newly built homes was also part of a social policy agenda. Sweden introduced a more innovative reduced VAT rate for small repairs on bikes, shoes, leather ware, clothes and home textiles, with a view to encouraging re-use (Table 3.11).

Table 3.11. **Changes to reduced VAT rates introduced in 2016**

	General	Food	Hotels/ restaurants	Newspapers/ e-books	Culture	Other
Rate ⇧ or scope ⇩	NOR		AUT		AUT SWE*	AUT BEL GRC
Rate ⇩ or scope ⇧		HUN PRT SVK TUR	CZE HUN PRT	CZE CHE NOR		HUN SWE TUR

* In Sweden, the increase in the rate for cinema tickets was legislated in 2015 but entered into force in 2017.

Source: OECD Annual Tax Policy Reform Questionnaire.

A number of countries also expanded the scope of their reduced VAT rates to support specific industries. Lower VAT rates on restaurant services were introduced in Hungary, Portugal and the Czech Republic. The Czech Republic also lowered the VAT rate from 15% to 10% on newspapers and journals, an industry which has been hit by declining sales. Norway and Switzerland introduced reduced VAT rates for online media. For EU countries, the situation is different as current rules allowing Member States to tax newspapers and publications at reduced rates are still restricted to printed publications and exclude online media. Finally, Turkey introduced several new reduced VAT rates including on a number of apparel and textile manufacturing products to support the sector.

Countries introduced reforms with a view to easing small business operations

Many countries raised their VAT registration or collection thresholds. OECD countries have very different rules regarding VAT thresholds (Figure 3.17). The main reason for excluding small businesses (and this notion varies considerably across countries) is that the costs for the tax administration of having all businesses pay VAT may be disproportionate compared to potential VAT revenues and that compliance costs for small businesses may also be disproportionate compared to their turnover. Based on those arguments, VAT registration or collection thresholds were raised in Belgium, Estonia, Finland, France, Hungary, Luxembourg, Poland and the United Kingdom. In addition, Sweden – which did not have a threshold

Figure 3.17. **VAT registration or collection thresholds on 1 January 2017 in USD**

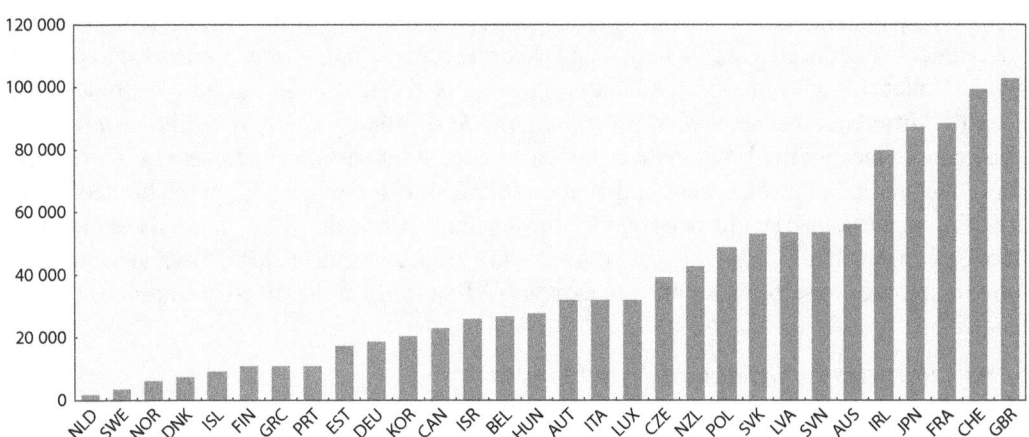

Note: No VAT thresholds in Chile, Mexico, Spain and Turkey

Source: OECD (2016c), Consumption Tax Trends 2016.

– introduced one, removing the obligation for small entrepreneurs producing taxable supplies below SEK 30 000 per year to register as taxable persons for VAT purposes (Table 3.12).

Table 3.12. **Changes to VAT registration/collection thresholds introduced in 2016**

Country	Registration or collection*	Old threshold	New threshold	Entry into force
Belgium	C	EUR 15 000	EUR 25 000	1 January 2016
Estonia	R	EUR 16 000	EUR 40 000	1 January 2018
Finland	R	EUR 8 500	EUR 10 000	1 January 2016
France**	R	EUR 82 200	EUR 82 800	1 January 2017
France**	R	EUR 32 900	EUR 33 200	1 January 2017
Hungary	C	HUF 6 000 000	HUF 8 000 000	1 January 2017
Luxembourg	C	EUR 25 000	EUR 30 000	1 January 2017
Poland	R	PLN 150 000	PLN 200 000	1 January 2017
Sweden	R	No threshold	SEK 30 000	1 January 2017
United Kingdom	R	GBP 82 000	GBP 83 000	1 April 2016

* Registration thresholds relieve suppliers from both the requirement to register for VAT and to collect the tax. Collection thresholds require taxpayers, even those below the threshold, to register for VAT, but relieve them from collecting VAT.

** France has two thresholds, one for commercial sales and furnished accommodation and the other for services and *professions libérales*.

Source: OECD Annual Tax Policy Reform Questionnaire.

Additional measures aimed at reducing compliance costs, in particular for smaller firms, were adopted or announced. Cash accounting for small companies became effective in the Slovak Republic in 2016. Similarly, Finland introduced cash-based accounting on VAT payments for companies with a turnover below EUR 500 000 as of 1 January 2017, which means that businesses under this threshold have the option to report and remit VAT only once they receive payments from their customers. The aim of this measure is to improve small companies' liquidity. Mexico introduced a measure on the recovery of expenses and investments during firms' pre-operative period of activities which allows them to recover their VAT payments a month after such expenses were made. In the United Kingdom, the government announced changes to the VAT flat rate scheme but those are intended to prevent abuse. Under this scheme, small businesses pay a fixed rate of VAT to the government and keep the difference between what they charge their customers and pay to the government. They cannot reclaim the VAT on their purchases except for certain capital assets. The reform plans the introduction of a new and higher 16.5% rate for businesses with limited costs, affecting in particular labour-intensive businesses that spend very little on goods, set to enter into force in April 2017. The measure is expected to reduce incentives for firms and agencies to move employees to self-employment to exploit VAT simplification aimed at small businesses.

Some countries reported anti-fraud measures

A number of countries reported the adoption of anti-fraud measures. Austria, the Czech Republic and the Slovak Republic introduced a number of measures to fight against VAT fraud, which came into force in 2016. In an effort to fight against tax evasion, Italy introduced quarterly VAT filing obligations on 1 January 2017. In Poland, a significant package of anti-fraud measures also became effective in January 2017. The package includes, among other measures, increased penalties for incorrect VAT settlements, the extension of the domestic reverse charge mechanism (i.e. shifting the obligation to declare and pay VAT from the supplier to the purchaser) in sectors subject to high risks of fraud (i.e. construction services, processors, gold and silver), and the introduction of joint or several VAT liability which implies that a person registering taxpayers for VAT purposes may be held jointly liable for VAT arrears (limited to PLN 500 000) for up to six months after registration. Latvia also introduced domestic reverse charge for transactions of precious metals and supplies of cereals and industrial crops as well as for mobile phones, laptops and tablets, confirming the increasing adoption of the domestic reverse charge mechanism in sectors highly subject to fraud that was identified last year.

VAT Revenue Ratios (VRRs) suggest that there is still potential to raise additional revenue by improving the performance of VAT systems. The VRR provides a comparative measure of how the tax administration's efficiency as well as exemptions and reduced rates affect VAT revenues. The VRR is the ratio between the revenue actually collected from VAT and the revenue that would be raised if the standard VAT rate were applied uniformly to the entire potential tax base (i.e. all final consumption) and perfectly administered and enforced. As shown in Figure 3.18, VRRs vary across countries. In the OECD, the average VRR remained relatively stable at 0.56 in 2014, compared to 0.55 in 2012, meaning that 44% of the potential VAT revenue is not collected. Although VRRs have to be interpreted with caution and tax base erosion may be caused by a variety of factors, these VRR estimates suggest that there is significant room in many OECD countries for raising additional revenues by improving VAT systems' performance through base broadening and better tax enforcement.

Figure 3.18. **VAT Revenue Ratios in OECD countries in 2012 and 2014**

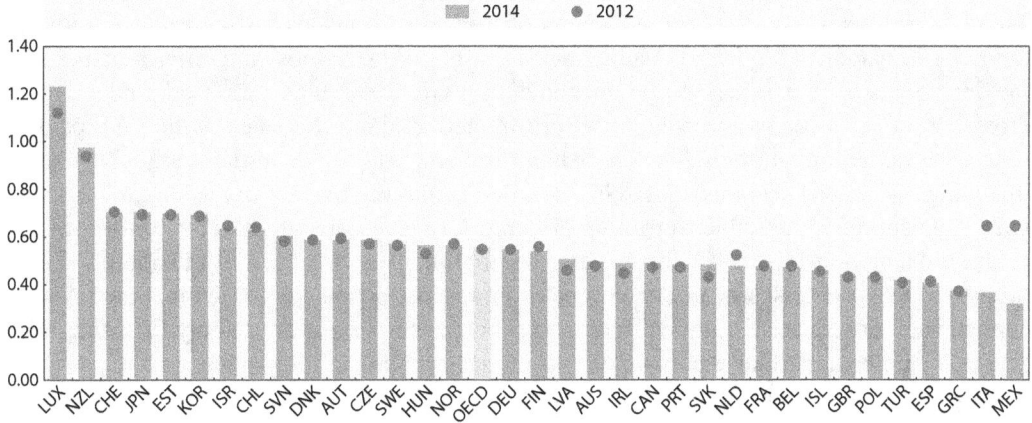

Note: The VRR for Luxembourg has constantly increased since the late 1990s and is now above the theoretical maximum of 1. The position of Luxembourg as a financial centre and a hub for European e-commerce has strongly contributed to its high VRR (for a more detailed explanation, see OECD (2016c) *Consumption Tax Trends 2016*)

Source: Consumption Tax Trends 2016, http://dx.doi.org/10.1787/ctt-2016-en.

Significant reforms and reform plans were aimed at enhancing taxation in the digital sector

The OECD International VAT/GST Guidelines (the "Guidelines") were endorsed by more than a hundred jurisdictions in November 2015 and incorporated into an OECD Recommendation by the OECD Council in September 2016. As discussed in the previous edition of this report, the elements of the Guidelines which received most attention were the recommended rules and mechanisms for the effective collection of VAT on business-to-consumer (B2C) supplies of services and intangibles (including digital supplies) by foreign suppliers. The Guidelines recommend that the right to tax these supplies for VAT purposes be allocated to the country where the customer has its usual residence and that foreign suppliers of these services and intangibles register and remit VAT in the country of the customer's usual residence. The Guidelines also recommend the implementation of a simplified registration and compliance regime to facilitate compliance for foreign suppliers.

In 2016, the implementation of the OECD International VAT/GST Guidelines continued. New Zealand introduced a new regime for the collection of GST on the supply of remote services by foreign suppliers which entered into force on 1 October 2016 and Australia enacted a similar regime for the collection of GST on digital products by foreign suppliers, which will come into force in July 2017. Both reforms are aimed at implementing the rules and mechanism recommend by the Guidelines. In addition, a number of non-OECD jurisdictions, including for instance India, Russia and Taiwan, have either aligned, or announced that they will align, their tax rules on cross-border supplies of services and intangibles with the Guidelines.

The European Commission also presented a number of measures as part of its Digital Market Strategy and its Action Plan on VAT to support the growth of online businesses, in particular start-ups and SMEs. New rules are proposed allowing companies that sell goods online to take care of all their VAT obligations in the EU through a digital online portal ("One Stop Shop"), hosted by their own tax administration and in their own language. These rules already exist for online sellers of electronic services, in accordance with the OECD International VAT/GST Guidelines. To support start-ups and micro-businesses, the introduction of a yearly VAT threshold of EUR 10 000 is proposed under which cross-border sales for online companies are treated as domestic sales, with VAT paid to their own tax administration. This goes hand in hand with other initiatives such as same invoicing and record keeping rules. This is aimed at making trading in the single European market as similar as possible to trading at home for these companies. The removal of the existing exemption from VAT for imports of small consignments from outside the EU is proposed, to tackle risks of unfair competition and distortion for EU companies. Also a change is proposed to existing VAT rules to enable Member States to apply the same VAT rate to e-publications like e-books and online newspapers, as they apply to their printed equivalents. These new rules are expected to have a major effect for companies selling goods and services online, as they will be able to benefit from fairer rules, lower compliance costs and reduced administrative burdens. Member States and citizens are expected to benefit from additional VAT revenues of EUR 7 billion annually and a more competitive market in the EU (European Commission, 2016).

Australia has announced the extension of its GST to low-value imports. The reform was announced in 2016 and, if adopted, will come into force on 1 July 2017. This reform is intended to even the playing field between imported goods valued at or under AUD 1 000, which are currently exempted from GST, and goods sold domestically that are currently subject to GST. Foreign suppliers, including "Electronic Distribution Platforms", that supply more than AUD 75 000 of taxable goods to consumers connected with Australia per year, will be required to register in Australia if the proposed reform is implemented. They will then be required to charge GST on their sales to Australia.

Excise duties were raised in many countries, in particular on tobacco products

In 2016, countries reported numerous excise duty increases. This section does not cover energy excise duties and taxes on motor vehicles (for these taxes, see Section 3.4). Table 3.13 shows that 16 countries reported increases in excise duties on alcohol and/or tobacco taking effect in 2016 and 11 countries reported increases entering into force in 2017 or later. The main goals behind these excise duty increases included raising revenue and improving health. In a small number of cases, increases were aimed at ensuring conformity with EU rules (e.g. Luxembourg, Czech Republic and Slovak Republic). Very few countries reported decreases in excise taxes. One example was the United Kingdom which froze the duty on beer, cider and whisky in 2016.

Table 3.13. **Excise tax increases on alcohol and tobacco products introduced in 2016**

Into effect in	Rate/Base ⇧	
	2016	2017 or later
Alcohol	ESP EST GRC NLD TUR ZAF	EST ISL PRT SWE
Tobacco	ARG AUS BEL CZE ESP EST FIN GBR HUN IRL LUX NLD SVK TUR ZAF	AUS EST GRC HUN ISL LUX LVA PRT SVK SVN

Source: OECD Annual Tax Policy Reform Questionnaire.

A large number of countries increased excise duties on tobacco products. Twenty countries reported excise duty increases for tobacco products taking effect in 2016 or later, against 9 countries for alcoholic products. The significant level of consumption, the relatively low elasticity of demand for tobacco products and the small number of producers have made tobacco taxation a particularly attractive way to raise revenues. Evidence on the health consequences of tobacco consumption and on the effectiveness of taxes to reduce tobacco use have also strengthened the case for increased tobacco taxation (OECD, 2016c). According to the latest figures, the total tax burden on cigarettes is now above 50% of consumer prices in almost all OECD countries and has reached 80% or more in 10 countries (OECD, 2016c).

In Greece, new consumption taxes on e-cigarettes and coffee were introduced. These taxes are similar to excise duties and became effective on 1 January 2017. The e-cigarette tax applies to e-liquids used in electronic cigarettes at an amount of EUR 0.10 per ml. The tax on coffee applies to coffee and preparations with extracts or concentrates of coffee at an amount varying between EUR 2 and EUR 4 per kg depending on the product. A new e-cigarette tax was also introduced in Finland.

Health-related taxes are becoming increasingly popular

Health-related taxes on food and non-alcoholic beverages have historically been rare but this decade has seen increasing interest in the use of such taxes. These taxes are generally implemented with the objective of raising revenue and changing consumer behaviour as evidence of the negative effects of unhealthy diets has become more prevalent. Indeed, there is now strong evidence that the excess consumption of products high in sugar, salt and saturated fats have negative impacts on long-run health outcomes (WHO, 2015). Most commonly, taxes have been imposed on sugar-sweetened beverages, although other products with high sugar, salt or fat content – such as chocolate, confectionary and ice cream – are also often taxed (Thomas and Brys, forthcoming).

In 2016, Belgium and the Netherlands increased their existing taxes on soft drinks. The Netherlands increased and reformed the rate structure of its tax on soft drinks. In Belgium, the tax on sugar-sweetened and artificially-sweetened beverages other than pure fruit and vegetable juices was increased in January 2016. The increase was part of a broader tax reform policy to shift some of the tax burden away from labour income and largely towards consumption that generates negative externalities (including diesel, electricity, alcohol, cigarettes, and stock market speculation). Initially, consideration was given to further differentiating the tax according to the health characteristics of beverages and some other food products, but so far the discussions have not resulted in any concrete measures.

A number of countries legislated or announced new taxes on soft drinks coming into force in 2017 or later. Portugal enacted a new tax on soft drinks based on the amount of sugar, effective as of 1 January 2017. South Africa announced in its 2016 Budget the introduction of a new tax on sugar-sweetened beverages. In the United Kingdom's 2016 Budget, it was announced that a tax will be imposed as of 1 April 2018 on sugar-sweetened drinks with total sugar content of 5 g or more per 100 ml, with a higher rate for drinks with 8 g or more per 100 ml. The tax will not apply to fruit juices or milk-based products, and smaller producers will be exempted from the tax. The revenue raised from the tax is proposed to fund sports activities in schools. Ireland has announced a similar tax in its 2017 Budget: the proposal is that it would apply to beverages with added sugar content of 5 g per 100 ml and above starting in 2018. In Spain, the government announced the introduction of a new tax on sugar-sweetened beverages, which will depend on the evolution of tax revenues. Finally, a tax on soft drinks was announced but has not yet been legislated in Estonia. Because these taxes are generally being introduced for the first time, many countries have planned a two-year period between the time when the measure was announced and their date of entry into force (Table 3.14).

Table 3.14. **Changes to excise taxes on soft drinks introduced in 2016**

	Base/Rate ⇧		New excise tax	
Into effect in	2016	2017 or later	2016	2017 or later
Soft drinks	BEL NLD			(ESP) (EST) (GBR) (IRL) PRT (ZAF)

Note: Countries in brackets have only announced reforms.

Source: OECD Annual Tax Policy Reform Questionnaire.

The only country that reported a tax reform related to other types of unhealthy products was Finland where the excise duties on sweets and ice cream were abolished. Concerns that the partial coverage of the tax on these products may have contravened EU state aid rules led to the removal of the tax. In general, in OECD countries, other more general health-related taxes have been less popular than product-specific taxes on soft drinks which are more easily identifiable, allow for easier sugar content targeting and have a generally readily available, affordable and healthy substitute (i.e. water) (Thomas and Brys, forthcoming).

3.4 Environmentally related taxes

Environmentally related taxes are defined as any compulsory, unrequited payment to general government levied on tax bases deemed to be of particular environmental relevance. Environmentally related taxes encompass all taxes that are likely to have a strong environmental impact – regardless of the reason why they were introduced – and cover a broad range of areas, including agrochemicals, energy, transport, waste, water abstraction and water pollution.

The rationale for introducing such taxes may differ and range from raising revenue to reducing environmental damage or recovering infrastructure costs. Generating government revenue has long been a major rationale for implementing environmentally related taxes, in particular for taxes on energy use. Taxes have also often been used as a cost-effective tool to mitigate negative environmental effects. By raising the price of environmentally harmful behaviours, they provide polluters with incentives to reduce their polluting activity. However, the potential for harnessing the power of taxes as an environmental policy instrument and for raising revenue remains large as environmentally related taxes are often set below the social costs of environmentally harmful behaviours. Gradually increasing environmental taxes could generate government revenue while mitigating negative environmental effects.

Environmentally related tax revenues vary widely across countries and are mainly driven by taxes on energy use and on motor vehicles

Revenues from environmentally related taxes in 2014 varied across countries, ranging from 0.06% of GDP in Mexico to 4.1% of GDP in Denmark (Figure 3.19). High revenues from environmentally related taxes can be the result of clear political efforts to reduce pollution but can also indicate limited pollution abatement. Between 1995 and 2014, environmentally related tax revenue measured as a share of GDP fell in the majority of countries covered in the report and remained stable in some of them. Revenues rose in eight countries, with particularly sharp increases in Estonia, Slovenia and Turkey. The latter two are now among the countries exhibiting the highest revenues compared to GDP. On average across the countries considered in the analysis, environmentally related taxes raised revenue

Figure 3.19. **Revenues from environmentally related taxes as a share of GDP by country in 1995, 2005 and 2014**

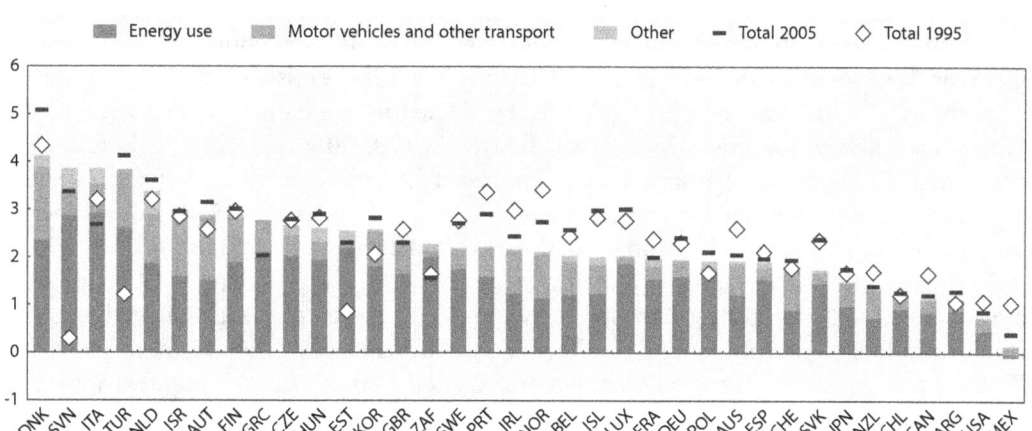

Note: Data for Poland are from 2013 (not 2014), Latvia missing.

Source: OECD Database on instruments used for environmental policy, http://stats.oecd.org/.

amounting to 2.2% of GDP in 2014, which is slightly less than in 2005 (2.4%) but equal to the revenue measured as a share of GDP raised in 1995 (2.2%).

Declining shares of revenues from environmentally related taxes in a majority of countries are likely due to at least four factors. First, environmentally related taxes usually take the form of excise taxes and real tax rate levels have not been maintained in all countries over time. Second, while high environmentally related tax rates may increase revenues in the short and medium term, they may lead to behavioural changes that result in a decrease in pollution or environmental harm in the long run, thereby reducing tax bases and possibly the revenues resulting from them. There is indeed considerable evidence that energy use decreases as a response to higher energy prices in the long run. Third, fuel demand may have been depressed by crude oil price hikes that directly affected fuel prices and slower growth in transport demand during the financial and economic crisis. Finally, other environmental policies may have overlapped with environmentally related taxes and reduced tax bases, e.g. by increasing fuel efficiency or decreasing distances driven.

Revenue collected through taxes on energy use accounted for more than 50% of total environmentally related tax revenues in all countries except Mexico in 2014. Taxes on energy use also drive changes in revenues from environmentally related taxes measured as a share of GDP over time in most countries. Motor vehicle and other transport taxes are the second most important category of environmentally related taxes in terms of revenues. Prior to 2010, motor vehicle taxes and other transport taxes were the most important source of environmentally related tax revenues in five countries (Iceland, Ireland, Israel, Norway and Switzerland), but taxes on energy use have recently become the first source of environmentally related tax revenues in these countries as well. Other environmentally related taxes are generally not a major contributor to public revenue.

Overall, environmentally related tax reforms in 2016 continued to focus on increasing taxes on energy use – particularly in the transport sector – and to a smaller extent on vehicle taxes. These developments are in line with past trends and will further increase the weight of energy taxes in environmentally related tax revenues. Taxes on transport fuels, in particular, have historically been widely used as a way to raise revenue, with tax rates and tax bases being consistently higher and broader than those on other types of energy use. This section suggests that negative environmental effects could be more effectively mitigated if tax rates better reflected the external costs of energy use in all sectors. Regarding vehicle taxes, reforms generally consisted in increasing taxes on conventional fuel vehicles and expanding tax exemptions for alternative fuel vehicles.

During 2016, a number of countries maintained momentum on climate preservation by increasing energy and carbon taxes and by slightly extending emissions trading.[6] However, more effort is needed to send effective price signals that induce carbon abatement and steer behavioural change towards a low-carbon future (OECD, 2016d). Figure 3.20 shows the proportion of CO_2 emissions from energy use priced at different effective carbon rate intervals across all countries covered by the present analysis (except Latvia) in 2012. Across all energy used in these countries, 85% of carbon emissions from energy use are not priced at a level reflecting a conservative estimate of their climate cost (EUR 30 per tonne of CO_2) and 42% are not priced at all (left panel). Except for road transport, carbon prices are currently too low resulting in limited incentives for cost-effective carbon abatement: only 4% are priced above EUR 30 per tonne of CO_2 and 54% are not priced at all (central panel). Countries aiming at preserving the climate by reducing carbon emissions from energy use could broaden tax bases beyond road transport and set higher (and more uniform) rates that reflect the climate damage from energy use, which would also generate additional government revenue.

Figure 3.20. **Proportion of CO_2 emissions from energy use at different effective carbon rate intervals in EUR per tonne, 2012**

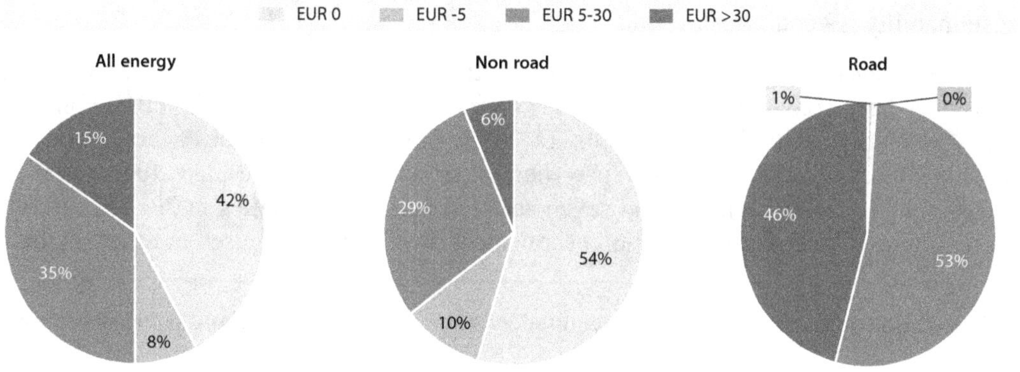

Legend: EUR 0, EUR -5, EUR 5-30, EUR >30

All energy: 42%, 8%, 35%, 15%
Non road: 54%, 10%, 29%, 6%
Road: 0%, 53%, 46%, 1%

Source: Adapted based on data from OECD (2016d), Effective Carbon Rates: Pricing CO_2 through Taxes and Emissions Trading Systems, http://dx.doi.org/10.1787/9789264260115-en.

Taxes on energy use played a predominant role in environmentally related tax reforms in 2016

The reforms that were announced and legislated in 2016 point to further increases in taxes on energy use, particularly in the transport sector (Table 3.15). Three countries (Estonia, France and South Africa) raised taxes on fuels across all sectors; ten countries raised taxes specifically on transport fuels; and seven countries increased taxes on energy used in other sectors including electricity production (Korea and Latvia), heating and process use[7] (Finland, Greece and the Netherlands) and electricity consumption (Norway and Sweden). Four countries explicitly reduced taxes on energy use (Denmark, Greece,

Table 3.15. **Changes to taxes on energy use implemented, legislated or announced in 2016**

	Rate/Base ⇧		Rate/Base ⇩	
Into effect in	2016	2017 or later	2016	2017 or later
Fuels, with sector specification:				
• Electricity production	KOR	KOR LVA (GBR[ca])	GRC NLD	GRC
• Heating and process	FIN[ca] GRC NLD	FIN FIN[ca]	SWE	GRC
• Transport	AUS[b] EST MEX PRT SWE	BEL EST FIN GRC ISL ISL[ca] MEX PRT NOR[ca] (EST)	SWE[b]	
Fuels, all sectors	EST FRA ZAF	EST (EST)	GBR	GBR
Carbon tax		CAN[alb] (GBR)		
Electricity consumption	NOR SWE	SWE	NLD	DNK SWE*

Notes: Countries in brackets have only announced reforms. **alb**: carbon tax in Alberta; **b**: tax related to biofuels; **ca**: tax based on carbon content of fuel.

* revenue is expected to increase through economic growth effects

Source: OECD Annual Tax Policy Reform Questionnaire.

the Netherlands, and Sweden) while real tax rates are expected to decline in the United Kingdom due to a freeze in nominal rates. Most of the countries that raised energy taxes implemented the reforms to raise revenue (13 countries) or to promote environmental sustainability (19 countries).

These developments are in line with past trends. Historically, tax rates on transport fuels have been consistently higher and tax bases consistently broader than those on other types of energy use (OECD, 2013; OECD, 2015). Figure 3.21 describes average effective tax rates (vertical axis) on energy use (horizontal axis) across the main fuel types and sectors in 34 OECD countries and seven selected partner economies in 2012. There is a clear difference between the taxation of transport fuels and energy used in other sectors.

Figure 3.21. **Taxation across all energy use (weighted average basis), 41 OECD and partner economies, 2012**

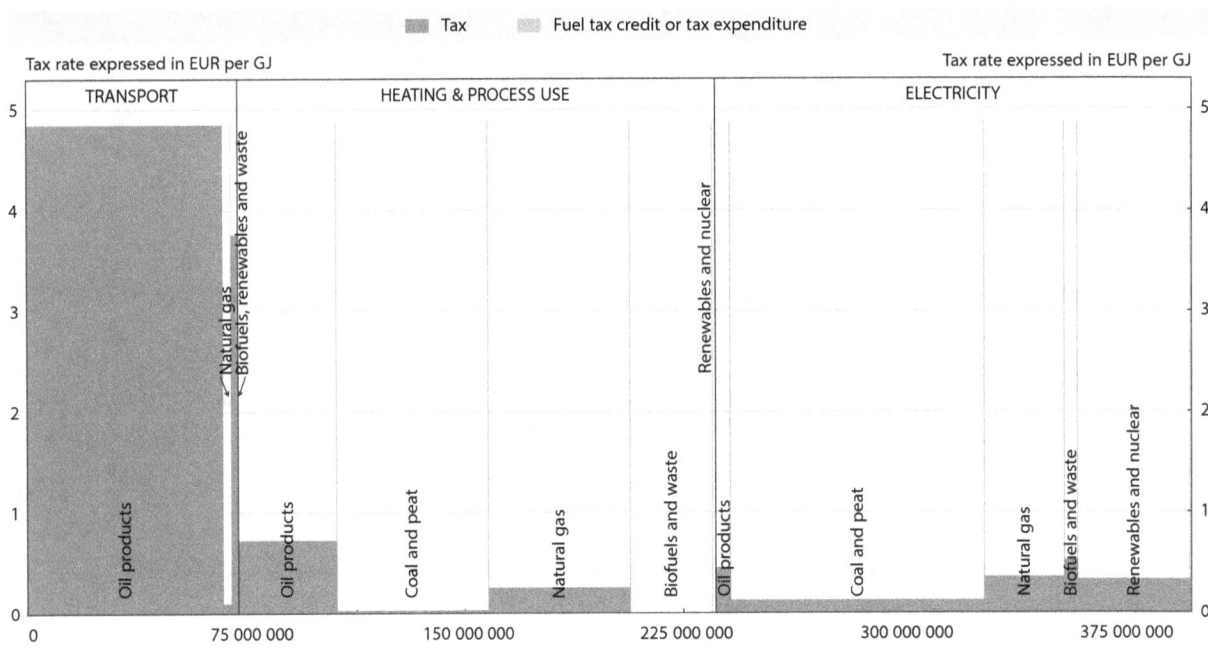

Source: OECD (2015), *Taxing Energy Use: OECD and Selected Partner Economies,* http://dx.doi.org/10.1787/9789264232334-en. The countries included are the 34 OECD countries (excluding Latvia) and Argentina, Brazil, the People's Republic of China, India, Indonesia, the Russian Federation and South Africa.

A better alignment of taxes with the environmental costs associated with energy use calls for higher taxes in most cases and for increased differentiation in some. Tax rates are particularly low on energy used in non-transport sectors and current rates do not properly reflect environmental costs. High transport tax rates have often been justified by the relative inelasticity of the tax base as well as the broader negative side effects of road transport on the environment (such as carbon emissions but also air pollution, accidents, congestion, noise and road wear and tear) but current rates are not aligned well with the strong variation of these negative impacts over time and place. Negative environmental effects from energy use can be more effectively mitigated when tax rates better reflect the external costs of energy use than they currently do (OECD, 2013; OECD, 2015).

Relatively low taxes on energy used in non-transport sectors can reflect distributional and competitiveness concerns. The distributional impacts of energy taxes differ by energy carrier and energy use. Flues and Thomas (2015) find that taxes on heating fuels are proportional to slightly regressive in most countries, whereas taxes on electricity are relatively more regressive. Policy makers have sometimes voiced concerns about potential losses of competitiveness as a result of unilateral action on energy taxes or carbon pricing. However, evidence shows that adverse competitive effects from carbon pricing do not materialise in the short run (Arlinghaus, 2015). Instead, stringent environmental policy can drive productivity (Albrizio et al., 2014a, 2014b) and thus tend to increase competitiveness in the long run. Often industries are exempted from fuel taxes if they are covered by an emissions trading system (ETS), although permit prices tend to be low and unstable.

Zooming in on tax reforms relating to specific fuels shows that reforms were often not in line with key principles of effective environmental taxation, but the picture is diverse. In some countries, tax reforms intended to treat fuels uniformly (e.g. Alberta's carbon tax ensures a uniform tax rate per tonne of CO_2 across fuels) or to harmonise the fuel excise regime (e.g. Estonia). Uniform taxes based on the carbon content of a fuel send equal incentives to reduce CO_2 across all energy users, a necessary condition for cost-effective emissions abatement. In other countries, however, tax reforms differentiated between fuels, with some countries further increasing the comparatively high taxes on oil products (e.g. Iceland, Portugal and Sweden) or further reducing the tax burden on natural gas and coal. For example, Greece reduced taxes on natural gas used in electricity production or for commercial and residential purposes and the Netherlands now provides tax exemptions for coal. Differential tax treatments of fuels may help raise more revenues but tend to go against the principles of effective environmental taxation if they do not reflect the negative environmental effects linked to the use of the fuels (OECD, 2013; OECD, 2015). These negative environmental effects can be multiple and often depend on how fuels are used.

Five countries implemented reforms targeting existing tax differentials between road transport fuels which favour diesel over gasoline use (Figure 3.22). Belgium implemented an advanced increase of excises on diesel while lowering those on gasoline. The overall revenue impact of the reform is expected to be positive. Estonia and Mexico increased tax rates on both fuels in 2016, but more strongly for diesel than for gasoline. France implemented a tax reform in 2014 that gradually harmonises gasoline and diesel taxes over five years. Finally, Hungary introduced a conditional excise duty rate increase – set to

Figure 3.22. **Effective tax rates on gasoline and diesel for road use, 2012**

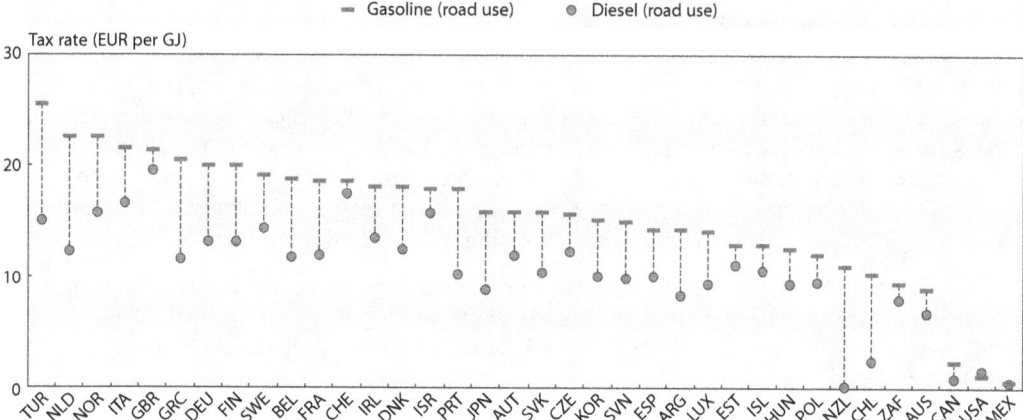

Source: Adapted based on data from OECD (2015), Taxing Energy Use: OECD and Selected Partner Economies, http://dx.doi.org/10.1787/9789264232334-en.

come into effect if the global price of oil reaches or drops below USD 50/barrel – which is higher for diesel than for petrol. Raising tax rates on diesel when they are still low better reflects the higher environmental costs associated with diesel use. Indeed, combusting diesel in vehicles emits higher levels of carbon dioxide per litre than gasoline and, depending on the technology employed, will often lead to the emission of more harmful air pollutants (Harding, 2014b). Fuel taxes should therefore be at least as high for diesel as for gasoline, even more so when diesel cars are more fuel-efficient so that a litre of diesel used results in more driving-related external costs (e.g. congestion).

In several countries, changes in taxes on energy use were part of more comprehensive reforms. For example, Finland increased taxes on energy use to compensate the revenue losses from reductions in other excise taxes (i.e. sweets and ice cream) and from maintaining tax exemptions for combined heat and power production. Mexico's reforms support a gradual liberalisation of fuel prices and aim at collecting taxes more efficiently. They are part of an overarching environmental tax reform (Box 3.7), which is evaluated comprehensively in Arlinghaus and Van Dender (2017). Finally, Estonia, Korea, the Netherlands and Sweden implemented broader energy tax reforms which are expected to have positive revenue impacts.

Box 3.7. Environmental tax subsidy reform in Mexico

While price regulation caused fossil fuels in Mexican energy markets to be sold at subsidised rates until mid-2014, Mexico recently moved away from transport fuel subsidies, increased tax rates on these fuels and introduced a carbon tax. Though motivations beyond environmental policy have played a role in Mexico, parts of the reform were explicitly motivated by environmental concerns.

More precisely, abolishing transport fuel subsidies and increasing taxes on transport fuels to much higher levels means that the prices of transport fuels now more closely reflect the external costs related to fuel use. Beyond transport, the new carbon tax covers a much larger share of emissions with a price, but the rates are very low and do not consistently reflect the carbon content of the underlying fuels. In particular, of all rates above zero, coal for use by households, industry and electricity generation is taxed at the lowest rate despite the high external cost associated with its use, and natural gas is zero-rated. In that sense, the cost of emissions differs across economic sectors and this reduces environmental effectiveness. Compromises were made on this dimension to help ensure overall political support for the reform.

The Mexican reforms significantly improve the extent to which the external costs of energy use are reflected in prices and increase government revenues, both welcome developments from an environmental and public finance perspective. Mexican taxes on energy, and in particular the carbon tax, may have the potential to raise much larger amounts of revenue if rates were increased, and the tax base enlarged in the future. The gradual transition towards higher taxes had initially facilitated the political acceptability of the reform and reduced the immediate distributional effects, but, as price deregulation progresses further, more attention may need to be devoted to analysing and addressing the distributional effects of these policies.

The Mexican reforms took place in a country with a decade-long history of fuel subsidies, and strong reliance on income from oil exports. Implementing an environmental tax reform in this context involves a considerable policy effort, insights from which could be relevant for a wider set of countries.

Source: Arlinghaus, J. and K. Van Dender (2017), "The environmental tax and subsidy reform in Mexico", *OECD Taxation Working Papers*, No. 31.

Taxes on motor vehicles and other transport taxes are the focus of reform in some countries

Some countries implemented tax reforms in the area of recurrent vehicle taxes and one-off registration taxes (Table 3.16). Most reforms were related to vehicle taxes that are levied periodically on vehicle ownership and use. Five countries increased tax rates on vehicles (Finland, Latvia, Portugal, South Africa and Turkey) and Iceland reduced tax reliefs granted to vehicles used by car rental companies following OECD recommendations, whereas three countries reduced vehicle tax rates or bases (Latvia, Norway and Turkey). The tax reductions compensated for an increase in other vehicle taxes in Latvia and in the carbon tax on transport fuels in Norway. Registration taxes, payable once when the vehicle is put into service, were raised in two countries (Greece and Portugal) and lowered in three countries (Denmark, Finland and the Netherlands). Most countries cite as rationales for the reforms environmental protection or increasing revenues when taxes were raised and equity concerns when taxes were lowered. From an environmental viewpoint, high registration taxes are likely to reduce the number of new vehicles purchased, but may also have adverse environmental effects when older, more polluting vehicles are driven for a longer period of time, increasing their share in a country's vehicle stock (OECD, 2016c).

Table 3.16. **Changes to taxes on motor vehicles and other transport taxes implemented, legislated or announced in 2016**

Into effect in	Rate/Base ⇧		Rate/Base ⇩	
	2016	2017 or later	2016	2017 or later
Vehicle tax	FIN* ISL TUR ZAF	LVA* PRT	HUN TUR	LVA* NOR**
Registration tax	GRC PRT	(EST GBR)	HUN FIN*	DNK NLD*
Vehicles running on alternative fuels			DNK HUN TUR	LUX SWE
Company cars		LUX	HUN	NLD*
Other (e.g. luxury cars, scrappage schemes, purchase support)	GRC	LVA	GRC HUN TUR	AUS

Notes: Countries in brackets have only announced reforms.

* no impact in total revenue expected

** part of a tax shift towards carbon content in automotive fuels (cf. Table 3.15).

Source: OECD Annual Tax Policy Reform Questionnaire.

Tax exemptions for cars that run on alternative fuels are more widely applied. Five countries provided new or extended existing tax rebates or full tax exemptions to vehicles that run on alternative fuels (e.g. hydrogen or electricity) or to hybrid cars to promote environmental sustainability. Those countries expect negative effects on tax revenues (Denmark, Hungary, Luxembourg, Sweden and Turkey). Overall, 19 OECD countries had such policies in place in 2016 (OECD, 2016c). Differentiating motor vehicle taxes according to fuel-efficiency and the emissions of a vehicle can provide incentives to switch to less polluting vehicles, but OECD (2009) shows significant variations in tax design across countries. Focusing only on fuel efficiency or CO_2 emissions when designing vehicle taxes can stimulate the sale of diesel vehicles that often emit additional harmful air pollutants (OECD 2016e).

The tax treatment of privately used company cars was modified in Luxembourg and the Netherlands. Luxembourg changed the valuation of the benefit associated with the use of a company car for personal purposes, and which is treated as taxable income to the employee, basing taxation on the valuation of the benefit in kind. In addition, Luxembourg increased taxes by a progressive rate depending on the CO_2 performance of vehicles. The Netherlands lowered the taxable benefit from the private use of company cars. Harding (2014a) finds that employee compensation in the form of personal company car use is effectively taxed more lightly than cash wages in most OECD countries, because tax systems tend to underestimate the value of the personal benefit associated with the private use of a company car. Such tax incentives encourage the use of cars over other modes of transport and create negative effects through increased driving (e.g. air pollution, carbon emissions, noise and congestion) which are discussed further in Roy (2014).

More comprehensive vehicle tax reforms were implemented in Latvia, the Netherlands and Norway, with expected positive revenue effects in Latvia. The Netherlands aimed at decreasing the dependence of tax revenues on CO_2 emissions and at simplifying current vehicle taxation. Norway decreased the annual motor vehicle tax for passenger cars to compensate car owners for an increase in tax rates on diesel and petrol used in transport (Table 3.15) following a parliamentary agreement on a green tax shift and expecting a slight decrease in revenues from this shift. Other more targeted reforms in motor vehicle and transport taxation were reported by Australia, Greece, Latvia and Turkey generally for either equity or revenue raising reasons. These reforms relate to abolishing luxury car reliefs or vehicle scrappage schemes and to implementing vehicle purchase support or road user fees.

Other environmentally related taxes are rarely affected by tax reform in 2016

Only very few countries reported reforms in other environmentally related taxes and sectors varied widely. Countries that reported reforms included Finland (increase in waste tax), Latvia (increase in tax rate and broadening base on natural resources), Norway (new tax on air passengers), Poland (new tax on the extraction of hydrocarbons), Sweden (new tax on chemicals) and South Africa (new tyre levy, increased levy on light bulbs and on plastic bags). Other environmentally related taxes were reduced in Denmark for competitiveness reasons (reduced tax rate on nitrogen oxides) and in Turkey to promote investment (tax exemptions for heat insulation and energy savings in buildings) (Table 3.17).

Table 3.17. **Changes to other environmentally related taxes implemented, legislated or announced in 2016**

	Rate/Base ⇑		Rate/Base ⇓	
Into effect in	2016	2017 or later	2016	2017 or later
Chemicals		SWE		
Natural resources	POL	LVA		
Waste	FIN			
Other	NOR ZAF	ZAF	DNK, TUR	

Source: OECD Annual Tax Policy Reform Questionnaire.

3.5 Property taxes

Property taxes account for a small share of tax revenues on average

Countries impose a variety of taxes on property. The most prominent property taxes are recurrent taxes on immovable property, which are typically a key source of revenue for local governments. Inheritance, gift and property transaction taxes are also common. A smaller number of countries impose a tax on some measure of net wealth. Nevertheless, property taxes tend to account for a small share of total tax revenues. Even if property tax revenues varied quite widely across countries, from 0.3% of GDP in Estonia to 4.1% of GDP in the United Kingdom in 2015, they accounted for only 1.9% of GDP and 5.6% of total tax revenues on average in the OECD in 2014 (Figure 3.23).

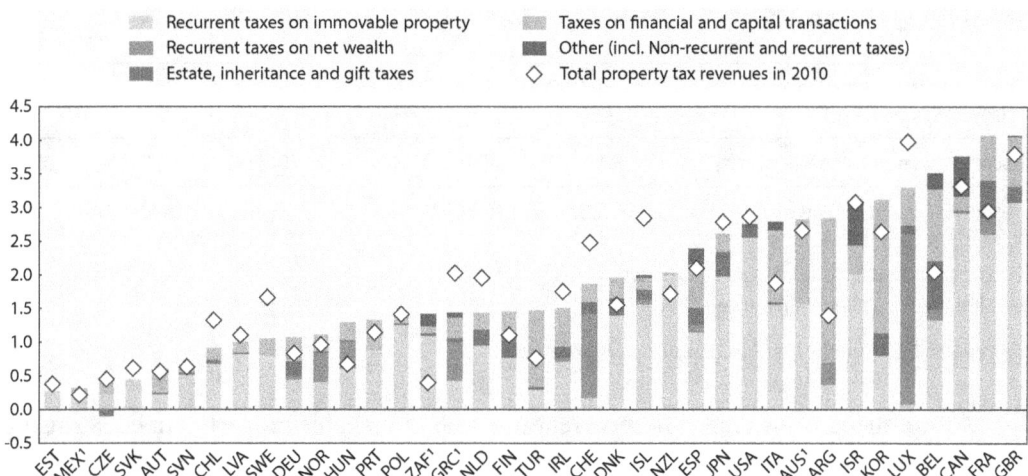

Figure 3.23. **Property tax revenues as a share of GDP by country in 2000 and 2015**

Note: 2014 used data for Australia, Greece, Mexico and South Africa.
Source: Regional Revenue Statistics databases (www.oecd.org/tax/tax-policy/revenue-statistics-comparable-tax-revenue-data.htm).

Property tax revenues increased in a majority of countries compared to their levels in 2000. Revenues from property taxes as a share of GDP were higher in 2015 than in 2000 in 21 countries and lower in 16 countries. Some countries, including Argentina, Belgium, Turkey, Hungary, Italy, and South Africa, have seen significant increases in property tax revenues as a share of GDP. Importantly, higher property tax revenues can be the result of property tax reform but also of higher property values, in particular in real estate. On the other hand, the most significant falls in property tax revenues as a share of GDP between 2000 and 2015 were recorded in Chile, Iceland, the Slovak Republic and Sweden.

Property tax reforms were generally oriented towards tax increases

Last year, only a limited number of OECD countries reported property tax reforms. The trends were also unclear, with some countries raising taxes and others lowering them, except in the area of inheritance and gift taxes where three countries reported reforms which had the effect of lowering tax burdens. The lack of clear property tax trends reflected the fact that reforms were motivated by very different objectives, including revenue generation and containing housing prices when taxes were raised, or increasing households' disposable incomes when they were lowered (OECD, 2016a).

Compared to last year, there were more changes reported in the area of property taxes and reforms were often aimed at raising taxes. The taxes that were generally raised included recurrent taxes on immovable property as well as transaction taxes on both movable and immovable property. Some of the reforms relating to real estate taxation sought to cool housing markets by targeting owners of multiple homes or buy-to-let properties (e.g. Israel, United Kingdom). On the other hand, most of the inheritance tax reforms lowered tax levels, through either base narrowing provisions or rate reductions (Table 3.18).

Table 3.18. **Property tax reforms that were implemented, legislated or announced in 2016**

Into effect in	Rate/Base ⇧		Rate/Base ⇩	
	2016	2017 or later	2016	2017 or later
Estate duties, inheritance and gift taxes		DEU ZAF	DNK IRL	DNK FIN GBR NLD**
Transaction taxes on movable and immovable property	AUT CHL GBR ZAF	BEL FRA		
Recurrent taxes on immovable property	FIN	FIN ISR PRT	ITA TUR	
Recurrent taxes on (net) wealth	ESP* LUX	ESP* LUX	NOR	NOR

* In Spain, the wealth tax was maintained.

** In the Netherlands, the reform was enacted in 2015 and became effective in 2017.

Source: OECD Annual Tax Policy Reform Questionnaire.

Most of the reforms related to recurrent taxes on immovable property aimed at raising them. Finland implemented a gradual increase in the maximum recurrent real estate tax rates in 2016 to boost municipalities' revenues. In January 2017, minimum tax rates were raised as well. Portugal introduced a new municipal property tax surcharge of 0.7% and 1% on real estate of a total taxable value respectively above EUR 600 000 and EUR 1 000 000. This surcharge, which replaces the stamp duty on residential urban properties or land for construction of a taxable value above EUR 1 million, aims at enhancing fairness. The reform also introduces a single rate of 0.4% levied on companies' total real estate. Israel introduced a new tax which became effective on 1 January 2017 to lower the demand for housing as an investment and cool the property market: owners of three or more apartments or houses are subject to a 1% tax on the value of those properties. In other countries, reforms were aimed at limiting the tax burden on homeowners: Denmark froze the land tax both for 2016 and 2017 to avoid tax increases on homeowners and Italy abolished its property tax for local services (TASI) on primary residences to raise the disposable incomes of workers and pensioners who are homeowners. Finally, Turkey introduced a five-year exemption from real estate taxation for buildings constructed within the scope of the investment incentive.

Transaction taxes on immovable property were raised in all the countries that reported tax reforms in this area. Austria changed the tax base for unremunerated real estate transfers within families from a favourable cadastre value to the market value. In addition, in the case of unremunerated real estate transfers, the flat tax rate was replaced with a three-bracket schedule depending on transaction values. In the United Kingdom, a rise in stamp duties on additional residential property became effective on 1 April 2016. Stamp duties on additional residential property are now charged at rates which are 3 percentage points higher than stamp duties on main residences. Those higher rates target purchases of second homes and buy-to-let properties. For commercial property, the structure of the stamp duty was also reformed so that the tax would be charged at progressive marginal rates, in the same way as residential property. A zero rate band was introduced and the new rates generally raise the stamp duty on the highest value commercial property, while reducing it for lower value property. In South Africa, an increase in the transfer duty rate on property sales above ZAR 10 million from 11% to 13% came into effect on 1 March 2016 with a view to raising additional revenue and increasing progressivity.

France and Belgium raised their taxes on financial transactions. In Belgium, the scope of the tax on stock exchange transactions was expanded to cover transactions ordered by a resident through a foreign intermediary. In addition, the tax ceilings were raised to twice their previous amount. These changes entered into force on 1 January 2017 with the objective of stopping avoidance through transactions channelled through foreign financial intermediaries. In France, the rate of the financial transaction tax, levied on acquisitions of shares issued by French listed companies with a market capitalisation exceeding EUR 1 billion, was increased from 0.2% to 0.3% as of 1 January 2017 and the scope of the tax will be expanded to include intraday transactions from 1 January 2018.

Several countries reduced taxes on inheritances and gifts. In Ireland, there was an increase in the capital acquisitions tax exemptions which took effect in October 2016. In the Netherlands, the exemption under the gift tax was nearly doubled for gifts intended for the purchase or the improvement of owner-occupied housing. In Finland, lower inheritance and gift taxes became effective on 1 January 2017. The gift tax threshold was raised from EUR 4 000 to EUR 5 000 and the maximum tax rate levied on gifts reduced from 20% to 17%. The tax rates levied on estates, meanwhile, were limited to 19% instead of 20%. The deduction from the value of the inheritance granted to the surviving spouse and lineal descendants under 18 was also raised. In parallel, however, the inheritance tax base was broadened by abolishing the tax exemption for life insurance proceeds. In the United Kingdom, the family-home allowance for direct descendants will be increased, with an additional nil-rate band increasing gradually to GBP 175 000 in 2020. The United Kingdom also reported a measure that will broaden the inheritance tax base by making UK residential property indirectly held by non-UK domiciled taxpayers using an offshore structure liable to inheritance tax.

Denmark and Germany introduced inheritance tax changes specifically addressing family business successions. In Denmark, the inheritance tax is being progressively lowered from its 2015 level of 15% to 5% in 2020 for business transfers to close relatives and business foundations. Germany adopted an inheritance tax reform after the constitutional court had ruled that existing rules privileged business owners. The reform seeks to strike a balance between equity objectives and the need to avoid excessive inheritance taxes on family businesses that would severely reduce their liquidity and threaten their existence. For inheritances up to EUR 26 million, the rules remained largely unchanged; it is still possible for business transfers to be up to 85% or even 100% tax-exempt if they satisfy criteria of job and wage preservation and business continuation (five years for the 85% exemption and seven years for full relief). The more significant changes relate to estate transfers above EUR 26 million, for which taxpayers may choose between a decreasing basic relief which leads to a reduction of the relief by 1% for each EUR 750 000 step above the EUR 26 million threshold, or a tax exemption if acquirers prove that they are not able to pay the inheritance tax with their own estate or the transferred assets. Overall, the revenue effects of this reform are expected to be very small.

South Africa introduced a new anti-avoidance measure targeting low-interest or interest-free loans made to trusts. The purpose of this measure is to address the avoidance of donations tax by individuals transferring their wealth through the allocation of interest-free loans to trusts. The new measure will deem the interest foregone to be a donation and the donor will be liable for donations tax on the deemed donation. The measure entered into force on 1 March 2017.

Spain and Norway reported changes to their net wealth taxes. In Spain, the wealth tax was extended for another year. More specifically, a 100% reduction of the wealth tax was introduced in 2008 but the tax was temporarily reinstated in 2011. Since then, the reintroduction of the 100% reduction has been repeatedly postponed for fiscal consolidation purposes. In Norway, on the other hand, as part of a broader tax reform aimed at boosting economic growth, the net wealth tax was lowered through a 10% reduction in the valuation of shares, operating assets and associated debts, and an increase in the basic allowance from NOK 1 400 000 to NOK 1 480 000 (double for married couples).

Finally, Luxembourg increased its minimum wealth tax on businesses. In 2016, Luxembourg repealed its minimum corporate income tax and replaced it with a new wealth tax on corporate entities' total net assets. In 2017, the amount of the minimum net wealth tax was increased from EUR 3 210 to EUR 4 815 for holding and finance companies with fixed financial assets, intercompany loans, transferable securities and bank deposits exceeding 90% of their total gross assets and EUR 350 000.

Notes

1. The total cost is estimated at EUR 3.5 billion (cash basis) and EUR 4.2 billion (transaction basis).

2. The net estimation of HUF 525 billion (around EUR 1.7 billion) does not reflect the tax cut's effect on payroll taxes paid by the public sector. The estimation is also static as it does not take into account the dynamic effects and revenue increases from the minimum wage increase.

3. The estimated net revenue effect of all tax reforms that came into force in 2016 is NOK (-) 5 260 million measured in nominal terms and (-) 5 360 million in real 2017 NOK. The estimated net revenue effect of the tax reforms that came into force in 2017 is NOK (-) 2 050 million. These are the accrued, annual revenue effects the first year the tax reforms came into force.

4. The rate is 15% for firms with taxable income not exceeding EUR 25000; for taxable income ranging between EUR 25000 and EUR 30000, the rate is set at EUR 3750 plus 33% (39% for 2017) of the taxable income exceeding EUR 25 000; if taxable income exceeds EUR 30 000 the rate is set at 18% (19% for 2017).

5. This report does not attempt to assess any country's compliance with the recommendations of the BEPS package, but merely highlights reforms that have been implemented, announced or legislated that may be BEPS-related. Whether or not a country is in compliance with a particular BEPS recommendation will be the subject of a separate process, which in the case of the minimum standards will involve a thorough peer review process. For more information on the progress of BEPS implementation please see OECD (2017c), "Inclusive Framework on BEPS: Progress report June 2016-July 2017".

6. Ontario in Canada passed legislation in 2016 to introduce an emissions trading system (ETS) in 2017.

7. The heating and process category includes energy used for industrial production and energy transformation as well as energy used for commercial and residential heating.

References

Albrizio, S., et al. (2014), "Do Environmental Policies Matter for Productivity Growth?: Insights from New Cross-Country Measures of Environmental Policies", *OECD Economics Department Working Papers*, No. 1176, OECD Publishing, Paris, http://dx.doi.org/10.1787/5jxrjncjrcxp-en.

Albrizio, S., T. Koźluk and V. Zipperer (2014), "Empirical Evidence on the Effects of Environmental Policy Stringency on Productivity Growth", *OECD Economics Department Working Papers*, No. 1179, OECD Publishing, Paris, http://dx.doi.org/10.1787/5jxrjnb36b40-en.

Appelt, S., et al. (2016), "R&D Tax Incentives: Evidence on design, incidence and impacts", *OECD Science, Technology and Industry Policy Papers*, No. 32, OECD Publishing, Paris, http://dx.doi.org/10.1787/5jlr8fldqk7j-en.

Arlinghaus, J. (2015), "Impacts of Carbon Prices on Indicators of Competitiveness: A Review of Empirical Findings", OECD Environment Working Papers, No. 87, OECD Publishing, Paris, http://dx.doi.org/10.1787/5js37p21grzq-en.

Arlinghaus, J. and K. Van Dender (2017), "The environmental tax and subsidy reform in Mexico", *OECD Taxation Working Papers*, No. 31, OECD Publishing, Paris, http://dx.doi.org/10.1787/a9204f40-en.

Brys, B., Perret, S., Thomas, A. and P. O'Reilly (2016), "Tax Design for Inclusive Economic Growth", *OECD Taxation Working Papers*, No. 26, OECD Publishing, Paris, http://dx.doi.org/10.1787/5jlv74ggk0g7-en.

Causa, O. and M. Hermansen (forthcoming), "The effectiveness of tax and transfer systems in reducing income inequality across OECD countries", *OECD Economics Department Working Papers*, OECD Publishing, Paris.

Ernst & Young (2017), "The Latest on BEPS – 2016 Year-End Review: A Review of OECD and country actions from July through December 2016", www.ey.com/Publication/vwLUAssets/EY-US-the-latest-on-beps-2016-in-review/$FILE/EY-US-the-latest-on-beps-2016-in-review.pdf (accessed 1 July 2017).

European Commission (2016), "Modernising VAT for E-Commerce: Questions and Answers", European Commission Fact Sheet, MEMO/16/3746, http://europa.eu/rapid/press-release_MEMO-16-3746_en.htm (accessed 1 July 2017).

Flues, F. and A. Thomas (2015), "The distributional effects of energy taxes", *OECD Taxation Working Papers*, No. 23, OECD Publishing, Paris, http://dx.doi.org/10.1787/5js1qwkqqrbv-en.

Hanappi, T. (forthcoming), "Measuring Effects on Tax Symmetry and Automatic Stabilisation", *OECD Taxation Working Papers*, OECD Publishing, Paris.

Harding, M. (2014a), "Personal Tax Treatment of Company Cars and Commuting Expenses: Estimating the Fiscal and Environmental Costs", OECD Taxation Working Papers, No. 20, OECD Publishing, Paris, http://dx.doi.org/10.1787/5jz14cg1s7vl-en.

Harding, M. (2014b), "The Diesel Differential: Differences in the Tax Treatment of Gasoline and Diesel for Road Use", *OECD Taxation Working Papers*, No. 21, OECD Publishing, Paris, http://dx.doi.org/10.1787/5jz14cd7hk6b-en.

Harding, M. (2013), "Taxation of Dividend, Interest, and Capital Gain Income", *OECD Taxation Working Papers*, No. 19, OECD Publishing, Paris, http://dx.doi.org/10.1787/5k3wh96w246k-en.

OECD (2017a), *Taxing Wages 2017*, OECD Publishing, Paris, http://dx.doi.org/10.1787/tax_wages-2017-en.

OECD (2017b), Secretary-General's Report to the G20 Leaders Meeting in Baden-Baden, Germany, www.oecd.org/tax/oecd-secretary-general-tax-report-g20-finance-ministers-march-2017.pdf (accessed 1 July 2017).

OECD (2017c), "Inclusive Framework on BEPS: Progress Report July 2016 – June 2017", www.oecd.org/tax/beps/beps-inclusive-framework-progress-report-june-2016-july-2017.htm (accessed 1 July 2017).

OECD (2016a), *Tax Policy Reforms in the OECD 2016*, OECD Publishing, Paris, http://dx.doi.org/10.1787/9789264260399-en.

OECD (2016b), *Taxing Wages 2016*, OECD Publishing, Paris, http://dx.doi.org/10.1787/tax_wages-2016-en.

OECD (2016c), *Consumption Tax Trends 2016: VAT/GST and excise rates, trends and policy issues*, OECD Publishing, Paris, http://dx.doi.org/10.1787/ctt-2016-en.

OECD (2016d), Effective Carbon Rates: Pricing CO_2 through Taxes and Emissions Trading Systems, OECD Publishing, Paris, http://dx.doi.org/10.1787/9789264260115-en.

OECD (2016e), "Car Purchase Tax: Green Reform in Israel", www.oecd.org/israel/OECDWorkingPaper-Green-Tax-Reform-in-Israel.pdf (accessed 1 July 2017).

OECD (2015), *Taxing Energy Use: OECD and Selected Partner Economies*, OECD Publishing, Paris, http://dx.doi.org/10.1787/9789264232334-en.

OECD (2013), *Taxing Energy Use: A Graphical Analysis*, OECD Publishing, Paris, http://dx.doi.org/10.1787/9789264183933-en.

OECD (2010), *Tax Policy Reform and Economic Growth*, OECD Publishing, Paris, http://dx.doi.org/10.1787/9789264091085-en.

OECD (2009), "Incentives for CO_2 emission reductions in current motor vehicle taxes", www.oecd.org/officialdocuments/publicdisplaydocumentpdf/?cote=env/epoc/wpnep/t(2009)2/final&doclanguage=en (accessed 1 July 2017).

OECD/KIPF (2014), *The Distributional Effects of Consumption Taxes in OECD Countries*, OECD Publishing, Paris, http://dx.doi.org/10.1787/9789264224520-en.

Piotrowska, J., Vanborren, W. (2008), "The corporate income tax-rate-revenue paradox: Evidence in the EU", *Taxation Papers*, European Commission, Brussels.

Roy, R. (2014), "Environmental and Related Social Costs of the Tax Treatment of Company Cars and Commuting Expenses", *OECD Environment Working Papers*, No. 70, OECD Publishing, Paris, http://dx.doi.org/10.1787/5jxwrr5163zp-en.

Thomas, A. and B. Brys (forthcoming 2017), "Designing Health-Related Taxes on Food and Non-Alcoholic Beverages", *OECD Taxation Working Papers*, OECD Publishing, Paris.

WHO (2015), *Using price policies to promote healthier diets*, World Health Organization, Geneva.

ORGANISATION FOR ECONOMIC CO-OPERATION AND DEVELOPMENT

The OECD is a unique forum where governments work together to address the economic, social and environmental challenges of globalisation. The OECD is also at the forefront of efforts to understand and to help governments respond to new developments and concerns, such as corporate governance, the information economy and the challenges of an ageing population. The Organisation provides a setting where governments can compare policy experiences, seek answers to common problems, identify good practice and work to co-ordinate domestic and international policies.

The OECD member countries are: Australia, Austria, Belgium, Canada, Chile, the Czech Republic, Denmark, Estonia, Finland, France, Germany, Greece, Hungary, Iceland, Ireland, Israel, Italy, Japan, Korea, Latvia, Luxembourg, Mexico, the Netherlands, New Zealand, Norway, Poland, Portugal, the Slovak Republic, Slovenia, Spain, Sweden, Switzerland, Turkey, the United Kingdom and the United States. The European Union takes part in the work of the OECD.

OECD Publishing disseminates widely the results of the Organisation's statistics gathering and research on economic, social and environmental issues, as well as the conventions, guidelines and standards agreed by its members.

www.ingramcontent.com/pod-product-compliance
Lightning Source LLC
Chambersburg PA
CBHW082353220526
45470CB00008B/2735